Climbing the
Corporate
Ladder

Climbing the Corporate Ladder

250 Top Tips for High Fliers

William Davies Ph.D.

Thorsons

An Imprint of HarperCollinsPublishers

Thorsons
An Imprint of HarperCollins*Publishers*
77–85 Fulham Palace Road,
Hammersmith, London W6 8JB

First published as *The High Flier's Handbook 1988*
This edition published 1991
3 5 7 9 10 8 6 4 2

© William Davies 1988

Cartoons by Tim Parker

William Davies asserts the moral right to
be identified as the author of this work

A catalogue record for this book
is available from the British Library

ISBN 0 7225 2533 8

Printed in Great Britain by
HarperCollinsManufacturing Glasgow

Contents

Read this first   7
Gaining altitude   9
Turbulence and dogfights   91
Cruising   133
Exercises   215

Read this first

Most books on management and personal effectiveness tell you *how* to do it. Some are written by people who have done well for themselves; these say 'This is what I did, look where it got me, it must be the way to do it,' overlooking the fact that people are different. What worked for them almost certainly will not work for you. If you are a quiet, shy individual, it is not helpful to be told that you need to bang the table at meetings to make your point, to storm around the office talking warmly to all and sundry, to organize riotous office parties. If you are outgoing and gregarious, it is not helpful to be told to spend 90 per cent of your time listening attentively to what others have to say.

Others are written by people who have *not* done well for themselves, but hope to do so by writing the book. Well, it is said the only people who made money out of the Californian gold rush were those who sold the picks and shovels, but this is taking it a bit far!

This book is different. It is a collection of concepts (ambition, blaming people, fear of failure), and words and phrases that people use ('anyway', 'for obvious reasons', 'I probably shouldn't say this, but . . .') that are relevant to anyone who is aiming high.

This is a short book, but even so, there are over 200 entries in it. You will act on only half a dozen of them at most. This means you are going to have to choose which bits you like, which you think might apply to you, which will benefit you. And maybe re-read it in a year and do the same again.

In other words, you are aiming to develop *yourself* significantly, to fulfil the potential you have. You are not aiming at some smug stereotype of a successful manager/person.

If you act on half a dozen entries, all well and good, but enjoy the rest, they are easy and entertaining to read. It is a list that I started compiling for my own private interest, but I hope that it now benefits and interests you too.

William Davies

Gaining Altitude

This section contains concepts and ideas which will help you get up to the level you set for yourself, and will do no harm even if you think you're in the jet stream already.

Ambition 11
'Anyway' 12
Appearance 12
Assumptions 13
Back scratching 14
Become a protégé 15
Being kept waiting 15
Blaming yourself 16
Brainstorming 16
Briefcase 17
Buying the Rolls 18
Charisma 19
Charm 20
Clear the desk 20
Clothes 21
Competence versus flamboyance 22
Compliments 23
Computers, technology and innovations 24
Confidentiality 25
Conserving intellectual effort 26
Copying the superstars 27
'Could do better' 28
Curiosity 29
Current affairs 29
Daydreams 30
Decisiveness 31
Doing the post 32
Do it now 32
Do what you want 33
The double act 33
Efficiency 35
Energy 36
Failings 37
Feedback 38
Filing systems 40

Fitness   40
Friends and enemies   41
Getting started   42
Goals   43
Go for it!   44
Have a nice day   45
Having a notepad handy   46
A high profile   47
Intelligence   47
Initiative   48
Introductions   48
Job changing   49
Keeping your own counsel
   50
Knowledge of your
   subject   50
Laughing at yourself   51
Let the good times roll   51
Listening   52
Meetings   52
Mistakes   54
Need   54
Negotiating   55
Nervousness   56
Numeracy   57
One at a time, please   58
'One suggestion would be
   . . .'   59
Ostrich imitations   59
Parading one's ignorance   60
Personal organizers   61
Perfection   61
Persistence   62
Perspective (having a sense
   of)   62
Planning   63
PR   64

Preparation   65
Priorities   66
Problem solving   66
Procrastination   67
Putting yourself forward   67
Relaxation   68
'Rightly or wrongly . . .'   69
Saying 'No'   70
Secretaries   71
Self-congratulation   72
Self-criticism   72
Self-efficacy   73
Self-examination   74
Setting your own standards   75
Sexism, racism, 'age-ism',
   etc.   75
Shutting up   76
Simplicity   77
Start with 'A's not with
   'C's   77
The streetwise versus the
   diplomat   78
Taking your opportunities   79
The 'to do' list   80
The telephone   81
Thinking   82
Time keeping   82
Time management   83
Threatened? Don't be!   84
Tone of voice   85
Undimensionality   86
Urgency and importance   87
Voice   88
What to do and how to do
   it   89
Your strengths and
   weaknesses   90

Ambition

Ambition, once decidedly out of fashion, is now more than acceptable, it's essential. After all, how will you become a high flier if you have no ambition? By accident? Who wants to employ people to whom things happen by accident?

However, there is one proviso – your ambition should not be of the personal, self-centred, conceited type that pays no heed to others' well-being. Acceptable ambition is where you have an awareness of your own good qualities and therefore know that you can do a high-level job well.

*See **Self-examination***

'Anyway'

Used in two ways:

• To disparage someone's achievements
• To excuse inaction.

In both cases the crucial phrase is, 'It would have happened anyway'. In real life, of course, things do not happen 'anyway'; good things generally happen by working and planning for them, bad things by negligence or lack of foresight.

It is important to recognize these facts and give credit to underlings for whom things seem to go right 'anyway', and look to oneself when things go wrong – it might *not* have happened 'anyway'.

Appearance

Your appearance really does count, especially in the early stages of someone getting to know you.

Get yourself to a reasonable weight, keep yourself moderately fit, and make sure you dress well. It matters.

Assumptions

Assumptions are okay as long as you know you are making them. Frequently, however, people base beliefs and decisions on assumptions that are so deeply held, or seem so reasonable, that they did not even realize that they were assumptions.

Keep a sharp eye out for your own assumptions tripping you up. Imagine yourself in the dock, maybe, in court, being asked, 'Why did you think that?'

See **Commonsense**

Back scratching

There is a saying 'You scratch my back and I'll scratch yours.' And indeed, *some* people do believe that one good turn deserves another. The operative word is, unfortunately, *some*.

There is another saying, 'Give him an inch and he will take a mile.' This one applies to the rest of the world. These are the people who, if you do them a favour, will ask you for another, and another, and another.

People fall into two types:

* Those who think that relationships should be in a balance
* Those who will take what they can get.

You need to learn to tell the difference between the two.

Become a protégé

Cultivate one or more people who you ask for advice. Not just advice on technical issues to do with your work, but to do with career decisions too.

Your habitual advisors come to feel that you are their protégé. The advantage of this is naturally that they have you in mind as someone they should do a favour for if at all possible.

Being kept waiting

Inevitably, all of us are kept waiting for some appointments: by dentists, doctors, colleagues, etc. *Don't* waste this time, and *don't* simply sit there getting stewed up that you are being kept waiting. What you should do is prepare something that you can do in that time – catch up on some reading, think about a particular project, meditate – anything as long as it's constructive.

Blaming yourself

Not a useful thing to do, it simply makes you feel bad.

When mistakes are made, high fliers extract the learning points, ready for next time.

See **Turning crises into opportunities** *and* **Feedback**

Brainstorming

A technique for generating possible solutions to an apparently insoluble problem. It requires the ability to relax, and then to jot down any possible solutions to the problem in question. The crucial element is to suspend your critical faculty *until* you have the list of solutions. If you are unable to suspend criticism, you are simply unable to generate a list.

Once you have the list, *then* evaluate each of the options, eliminating the impractical ones and expanding the practical ones. You then have a much shorter list, possibly only one, two or three items long, of *realistic* possibilities.

Although this sounds very easy, many people find it difficult to loosen up enough to produce a long list of possibilities.

You are running a two-day workshop on how to behave in meetings. It is due to start at 9.30 a.m. and it is now 8.30 a.m. You open up your briefcase to run quickly through again the notes, video-tapes, and other materials, only to find that, instead of the 'meetings' package, you have brought the folder on 'time-management'. All the participants for the course are staying in the same building as you, expecting the course to start in an hour. You are 220 miles away from your office, having travelled by car.

What are you going to do? Write down as many possible solutions as you can. Think freely. You should be able to generate at least 10 easily, but better still 20 or 30.

Briefcase

Only carry a small one, otherwise it looks as though the *papers* you carry round with you are more important than your ideas, personality and general talent.

Buying the Rolls

When you buy your first (used) Rolls-Royce you will probably try to save some of your hard-earned money by doing so privately through the small ads. You will probably try to knock the price down.

There are two approaches:

- You can prowl round the car suspiciously, pointing out every fault and minor flaw, then make your low offer
- You can appreciate the car fully, praise its condition, admire how well kept it is, *then* make your same, low offer.

The second one is better. If you try the first strategy, the seller will simply turn you down and wait for someone who appreciates the car to come along and make a good offer.

This applies not just to cars, and not just to buying things. First decide on your course of action (in this case the price you want to offer); second, be *sympathetic* to your client, patient, customer, or whoever. Demonstrate to them that you are on their side.

Charisma

An elegant research project revealed that there are
two components to charisma. Charismatic people
have these qualities:

- They share the same values as those who regard
  them as charismatic
- They are extremely effective in achieving the
  goals associated with those values.

At first sight, this analysis appears to miss out the
essential aspect of charisma. However, on further
thought, one realizes that most charismatic
people, for example, certain politicians, are not
necessarily charismatic in their early days; it is only
when one realizes how effective they are at
achieving their ends that one comes to regard
them as such.

If one is aiming at being charismatic, this simple
but effective analysis is well worth thinking about.

Charm

Charm is a very much underestimated quality; it is *not* essential to have it, but it is a tremendous advantage if you can develop it.

Examples of how charm can ease your passage through life abound, but one from the relatively recent past is the 1984 US Presidential election. If the pundits are to be believed, the content of President Reagan's thoughts and speeches was decidedly lightweight – it was his easy manner and substantial charm that won him a second term in the world's most powerful position.

Clear the desk

It is better to have a clear desk than a cluttered one, the reason being that it makes it much easier to concentrate on and complete the task in hand.

Just have the task that you are involved in on top of your desk . . . even if this means stuffing all the other papers into the drawers for the time being. As the saying goes, 'Out of sight, out of mind.'

Clothes

The way you dress has been shown to be important, particularly in your early meetings with new acquaintances. At that stage, you are well advised to wear whatever is the uniform for your particular occupational group; if the uniform is a suit, then wear a good suit, if it is jeans and a tee-shirt, wear *good* jeans and a *good* tee-shirt.

However, there is an interesting phenomenon that, once you have gained credibility with the people you work with and they know you are good at your job, you can gain further recognition by turning up in the *wrong* clothes for your group. So, if you are an industrial relations trouble-shooter and, wearing your usual immaculate suit, develop a reputation as a top class industrial relations trouble-shooter, you may subsequently appear in jeans and a pullover and not merely 'get away with it', but actually enhance your reputation. This is called *idiosyncratic credit*.

Competence versus flamboyance

You can go a very long way on competence alone, so long as you are *relentlessly* competent.

The same does not apply to flamboyance, but it can get you noticed or remembered, so long as you are competent as well.

Overall, boring old competence is much underrated . . . go for it! The common thread amongst those who get places is that they can jolly well do their job!

If you have other 'bolt-on' extras as well, so much the better, but don't concern yourself with them too much.

Compliments

Giving

Compliments are very good if they are subtle ones. If you compliment a person, then clearly in that person's eyes, you are an individual of very fine and sensitive judgement!

Some compliments are too gross, and are therefore taken as flattery which is usually counter-productive.

For example:

- Flattery 'You are, of course, a very intelligent person.'
- A *subtle compliment* 'Smith is a very nice chap, but probably not quite of the same intellectual calibre as most of the people that you and I are used to talking to.'

Those who master the art of subtle and deserved compliments are usually very well liked indeed!

Receiving

Accept them. If you can do no more, at least say 'thank you'.

Don't say, 'Well it just turned out well', or any other phrase which avoids accepting credit.

Computers, technology and innovations

Many people whose work does not involve technological innovations tend to write such things off. Don't. Even if they don't have a direct relevance to you, they will certainly have an indirect one. Okay, so there is no need to make discovering computers a top priority, but don't give up an opportunity to learn about such things. You could be surprised at what you learn.

Confidentiality

Confidentiality may be necessary in either *formal* or *informal* situations.

In *informal* situations, the more you treat information as confidential, the more information people will give to you, and possessing information rarely works to one's detriment, but often to one's advantage.

In *formal* situations you should work out what categories of information you can keep confidential. Therefore, when someone asks you whether a particular piece of information will be kept confidential if he tells it to you, you can explain exactly what the situation is. Better to do this than to give a blanket assurance of confidentiality (which will be seen through and anyway could put you in a serious dilemma if you are then told information which you *have* to pass on), or a simple assertion that nothing is confidential (which would discourage the person from talking to you further).

Conserving intellectual effort

Some people like to think that they should hold back their full intellectual effort for really important tasks, fearful that they will in some way 'use up' all the neurons banging around in their heads. Therefore, they hold back on some tasks, for example, memorizing what colleagues tell them about their families, for fear that it will occupy memory space which might be more profitably filled by something else.

This is nonsense. Give everything your all. It doesn't matter if you remember a lot of irrelevant information, there are an awful lot of neurons in that head of yours, and plenty of space for all the information you could possibly want. So what if you do 'waste' some effort – there is no joy to be found in an effort-free existence!

Copying the superstars

There is no set formula for a high flier. If you latch on to one particular high flier and try to copy him or her, you're probably letting yourself in for trouble. What works for them may not work for you, because yours will not be a perfect copy, and even if it *is* successful you may let yourself in for an undue amount of **stress** trying to maintain a façade.

It is much better to try and identify one specific quality that you have observed in a successful individual. If this fits in with your existing strengths, and is an easy quality to incorporate, then, by all means, try to build it in to your repertoire.

'Could do better'

'Could do better' is a phrase that some people were pleased to see on their school reports. It implies that the person is doing well enough already, but, if they chose to, could surge ahead of their contemporaries. It conjures up the notion of a powerful motor idling, yet still keeping up with the rest of the pack.

In later life, when no-one except yourself is writing your term report, things are different. To do really well, you need not only talent, but also the sustained effort to get the best from that talent. There are no plaudits for unused brain-power; *having* potential is not good enough, *achieving* your potential is the key.

Curiosity

Children tend to have a healthy curiosity across a range of areas which adults often lack, it having been replaced with concentration, application, specialization, etc.

If you look at successful people, however, one of the common threads is that they are curious, they are interested, they want to know how things work and how things are organized. It stands them in good stead, and it will stand you in good stead too. You must constantly learn lessons from one area that can be applied to another. Work on your curiosity, see if you can re-kindle and re-develop it.

Current affairs

One's knowledge of current affairs is widely regarded as a good measure of one's 'depth', 'breadth of interest' and general 'mental activity'. Try to develop and maintain your interest in current affairs.

Daydreams

Don't write off daydreams; they can be very constructive and useful.

At their best, they show you the direction that you want to go in and bring to life all the rewards that direction might bring you. They brighten you up and motivate you to work towards that special goal. At their worst, of course, they are unrealistic fantasies which you will never achieve and they simply serve to make you dissatisfied with your current situation.

Stick with your daydreams. Make them achievable, and make sure you ally them to hard work and perseverance. That way they stand some chance of becoming a reality!

Decisiveness

One of the things that ambitious people grasp is that they should be decisive, and it is perfectly true that it is better to be decisive than indecisive. However, the rush to impress others with one's decisiveness can lead to people performing rather like the screen stereotype of a decisive tycoon. Worse still, it frequently leads to a wrong, or ill-considered decision.

Take your time about making decisions, **consult** those affected and **persuade** others that your course of action is right. No-one is impressed by over-hasty decisions.

Finally, sometimes *it does not matter* which of two or more courses of action you decide upon. In this case, simply make an arbitrary decision, and then make sure you stick to it. The only danger with arbitrary decisions is that sometimes one does not feel committed to them; otherwise there is nothing wrong with them at all.

Doing the post

Set a good amount of time aside first thing in the morning specifically for going through your incoming post, probably with your secretary.

Reply to what you can immediately, before you open the next letter. Minimize what has to be dealt with later, and organize immediately how and when you are going to do those things – put them in your diary with a day *and* a time.

Do it now

Don't be misled by the fact that you have heard this one a million times before. It is the single most important rule of time-management. If you stick to it you will find a lot of the other rules follow automatically.

The only proviso: 'now' means just that. Not 'immediately after finishing this cup of coffee' . . . 'as soon as I've done this other thing' or anything else.

Do what you want

Even when you have properly set your **priorities** and got yourself organized as to what you should be doing, there are times when you simply don't feel like doing it, maybe because you don't feel up to it, thanks to a late night or two recently, or a heavy morning, or whatever.

Step one in this situation is to push yourself . . . see if you can make yourself feel up to it.

But if that doesn't work, don't simply do nothing. Choose a task you *do* fancy doing. It might not be your top priority, but it is (usually) better to do *something* than nothing.

The double act

This is a 'little gem' of a tactic, employed by those at the level above you. Here is an example of how it can work, in a hospital setting: You go to the medical director to request an additional member of staff, and his reply is that he must check it out with the administrator. This is perfectly reasonable, but you know from past experience that if you ask the administrator, he will reply that he must check it with the medical director. You're caught; neither will tackle the responsibility alone, and you are never able to get them together to discuss it jointly. You're well and truly stymied. The solution? You try to work out what the hidden message from, in this case, the medical director is. It will usually be one of these:

- 'I hear your request; give me time to think about it.' In which case, you should be gracious enough to allow him or her that time, but prompting in due course if it's been shelved.
- 'This isn't something I have jurisdiction over, I really do have to check it out with colleagues.' You can't ask fairer than this; your request has been heard, and in due course, it will be 'processed'.
- 'I don't like this idea, but I don't have the heart to tell you so, outright.' If you're sure this is the message you're getting, either give up (until another day!) or argue your case a little further if that is appropriate. But remember, however well you've made your case, your superior does have the right to vet, and, indeed, to veto, your ideas. This is a fact of life you have to accept without taking it personally.

Efficiency

Make no mistake, efficiency is wonderful, and to be preferred to inefficiency any day. Be wary, however, about becoming an efficiency freak, spending *too much* time organizing it to its best advantage. Remember that activity of almost any sort, even if it is not 100 per cent efficient, is most often better than inactivity.

Energy

One of the hallmarks of high fliers is that they do a lot of things – they are energetic. The more you do – the more energy you have – the higher you are likely to fly, so long as it is not simply 'frantic activity'. It is not enough simply to be energetic at the expense of **thinking** or setting priorities.

When in doubt, however, do something rather than do nothing. Thinking and sorting out your priorities are absolutely necessary to flying high, but they are not excuses for inaction. You can increase your energy level by:

- Realizing that 'energy' is not something that you are born with; if you increase your output, you are, by definition, more energetic
- Developing your **fitness**
- Minimizing and coping with **stress**.

Failings

There are two things you should do with your personal failings:

- You should be aware of them, so that you can steer clear of situations where they might be a big handicap to you
- You should try and work on them to minimize them or get rid of them.

What you should *not* do is dwell on them. It is said that none of us is perfect, and, for most of us, that is true!

Feedback

Negative

Negative feedback is telling people where they have gone wrong. It is necessary for two reasons:

- It lets people know where they are going wrong (they may think they are doing the task absolutely correctly)
- It lets people know that what they do is noticed.

The way of giving negative feedback is in two stages:

- You say *exactly* what the incorrect action was
- You say *why* it was incorrect and why you are displeased.

Be sure to emphasize that you are not displeased with the *person*, rather this particular *action*.

Positive

Positive feedback (telling people how well they have done) is good for two reasons:

- It lets the person know that what they did was the right thing to do
- They know that what they do is being noticed.

This keeps up their motivation.
- You make clear exactly what action was the good one
- You say why it is good and why you are pleased.

There is no harm in implying that you think the person concerned is also a pretty good all-round chap/chappess.

Getting positive feedback can be difficult, not so much because you have done nothing good but because either it does not occur to others that you need it or they do not think it is 'their place' to compliment you. Ironically, this means that the boss is often the person who receives least by way of compliments (positive feedback).

The way to get your share of positive feedback is simply to ask for it – in a subtle way of course, but not too subtle. There is nothing wrong with questions such as, 'What do you think were the best bits of that presentation . . . which bits do you think I should make sure to put in next time?' Or even just a straight request for feedback on an area you know you are strong on, resulting in simple questions such as, 'What did you think of that project I gave you last Friday?'

However you tackle it, be sure to realize that you are just as entitled to positive feedback as anyone else, and work out how to get it occasionally. It will make you feel better and work better.

See **Positive and negative control** and **Self-esteem**

Filing systems

Work out your own filing system. Don't let anyone else do it for you. Analysing information and sorting it into different categories are the basic processes involved in thought. Therefore, the system for categorizing and storing information – filing – is much too important to be left to somebody else.

Fitness

Two of the most obvious hallmarks of the high flier are firstly that they work hard for long hours and secondly that they take very little time off for sickness.

One therefore needs to realize that fitness does not necessarily come naturally to one, and needs to be worked upon. The essential ingredients for this are:

- *Diet* Make a point of having a nutritious but not over-calorific diet

- *Physical exercise* Aim for regular, frequent, but not over-taxing exercise. Swimming and cycling, but not competitively or against the clock, are ideal
- Cut down on stress
- *Sleep* Make sure you usually have adequate sleep. There will be times when you are not able to, so ensure you have your sleep reservoir well stocked.

See **Energy**

Friends and enemies

There is a simple rule here: You need as many friends as possible, and as few enemies. This has repercussions: it means that if you resign from a job, you should not tell your former boss where to stick it, no matter how much you would like to. This can spoil your fun.

On the whole it is more important to cut down your number of enemies than to boost the number of friends. You cannot always rely on friends backing you up, but you can be pretty sure an enemy will shoot you down!

Getting started

This is a problem that everyone has from time to time. You are aware that there are all sorts of things that need to be done, and you don't seem to be able to get it together to do any of them.

Four things to do:

- Forget all your time management rules ... prioritizing of tasks, 'do the worst task first', and so on. Just do what you fancy doing.
- Get up from where you are sitting (you are always sitting). Sit down again (there or elsewhere).
- Make the slightest start on the task. For example, just find the paper you need for the task. Once you have done that, it will be easier to carry on to the next stage, and the next, and so on.
- Once you have got your momentum back, revert to some sensible time-management rules!

Goals

When you begin to work out what your goals are, you should do so under two headings:

- Your personal goals
- Your work goals.

Under each you should have three goals as follows:

- Short term – today
- Medium term – within a month
- Long term – within a year or more.

There are only two rules for goal setting:

- You must do it regularly and frequently
- Your goals should be easily achievable. Remember, when you have achieved one goal you can set yourself another straightaway.

See Urgency and importance

Go for it!

Competence, hard work, organization, all these are absolutely vital, but you need a bit of a spark inside you as well . . . go for it!

See **Setting limits**

Have a nice day

The time to judge when you have had a nice day is, of course, at the end of it. When you reach the end of the day you probably make some kind of judgement or have some kind of feeling about whether it has been a 'nice day' or not. But you are probably not assessing your day on 'niceness' at all, what you are really doing is deciding whether or not your day has been a *satisfying* one, whether you have achieved the things that you wanted to achieve or whether you got sidetracked into other less important tasks.

The feeling you get at the end of the day is probably a better judgement of your work performance than the feeling you get as you go through it. What you therefore aim to do is to end up feeling satisfied, and feeling that you've achieved a fair proportion of what you set out to do. Of course there is nothing you can do about it once the working day is over, so you need to bear this in mind. Ask yourself 'Is what I'm doing now something that I'll be pleased to have done when I look back on the day?'

So, when someone says to you, 'Have a nice day', what they really mean to say is 'I hope you go through the day doing those kinds of things which will leave you satisfied at the end of it.' It's not quite so snappy though – and it'll never catch on!

Having a notepad handy

Some of the best ideas occur to you at the strangest times; driving a car, at a social occasion, late at night or early in the morning.

In order to capture these ideas and make sure they don't disappear as quickly as they came, you should ideally carry around a notepad and pen. If you can't bring yourself to consider this a good idea, then allocate a few pages of your diary or personal organizer especially for this purpose.

Whatever you do, make sure you write down those bright ideas and spend some time later following them up, either discarding them or putting them into practice. No matter how vivid the idea is at the time there is a good chance you'll forget it later on unless you've made a proper note of it. What is more, it's not good enough just to jot down a few random 'reminder' words; you need to note it down properly, so that if you come back to it later it will remind you of exactly what you meant when you wrote it.

A high profile

Taking a high profile means spending a lot of time talking or listening to people face to face, on the telephone, at meetings. That is all it is, just doing a lot of talking and listening, not necessarily in an extrovert or exuberant way, just a lot of it.

Whether or not you wish to take a high profile is of course another matter – sometimes you do, sometimes you don't. The reassuring thing is that anyone can do it if they wish; you just have to choose when!

Intelligence

High fliers can get away with any personality characteristic except stupidity. It is the kiss of death to become known as 'not that bright', 'a bit dim', or any other similar, disparaging phrase. In the Western world, the prejudice in favour of bright people is so deep-rooted that few people think of it as a prejudice at all.

Initiative

This one is a gem for true high fliers, for two reasons: First, it is essential to have it, and second, it is very difficult to develop or imitate it. It is different from, for example, a knowledge of **current affairs** which can and should be developed; initiative is something that, to a large extent, you either have or you do not by the time you are in employment.

*See **Unidimensionality***

Introductions

Introductions are over-rated. Develop contacts for yourself, if at all possible.

Job changing

There is nothing intrinsically wrong with changing your job frequently. Neither is there anything wrong with staying put. There are many examples of high fliers who have stayed put throughout their careers, equally there are many who have made frequent changes.

One word of warning, however. If you do change your job frequently, make sure you can defend yourself against allegations of being a dilettante. Few employers wish to employ someone who they suspect is going to leave them after only a year or so. On the other hand, a change of job every couple of years can give a striking impression of someone who is 'on the way up', as long as the change is always for the better!

Keeping your own counsel

A posh way of saying that you should keep a good number of things to yourself. Of course, you can be friendly with whom you wish; of course, you can be outgoing and enjoy yourself if you want. Just keep a good eye on what you give away. Not many high fliers are blabbermouths as well.

Knowledge of your subject

This one is in danger of being over-looked in the search for factors which might bring you instant success. There are no two ways about it though, an extensive knowledge of your subject is absolutely essential. When the chips are down, everybody will recognize and respond to expertise.

See **Expert**

Laughing at yourself

This is a 'Catch 22' concept. There are undoubtedly occasions where you *need* to laugh at yourself. On those occasions, you will certainly forget to do so.

Let the good times roll

Some people are good at learning lessons from their mistakes and that is a very useful ability to have.

However, how many of us ask the question, 'What lessons can I learn from my successes?'

Analyse the good times as much as you analyse your mistakes; try to see what were the antecedents or conditions of your successes. If you can get the conditions right to encourage more and more successes, you are going to have awfully few mistakes to analyse. You can probably live with that!

Listening

Learn how to listen. The high flier is not some kind of self-contained action pack; he or she needs to know all about the world around, and to distil and evaluate ideas from others.

Meetings

Their value

Meetings are regarded by some as good, by others as bad. As ever, the boring truth lies somewhere in between – some are good, some bad. The one fundamental rule is that the meeting must have a *purpose*, but the snag with this is that some purposes are subtle and sophisticated and are not made explicit. It is easy to grasp that a meeting to decide the venue for next year's conference has a clear purpose, but it is less easy to see what the purpose of a department's routine 'weekly meeting' might be. In fact, it may very well serve to cement **relationships**, and to boost the **self-**

esteem and commitment of those at the meeting. On the other hand it may not, it may simply be an irritant to all who have to attend. The skill of the manager is in deciding whether a meeting *really* has a purpose, and whether it is being achieved. Be aware that some meetings serve a useful purpose that is nevertheless kept hidden from the powers that be because it is too woolly.

Your performance at them

Get to grips with meetings – find out how to chair them; find out how to do yourself justice as a member. Others attach great importance to how you perform in meetings; the meeting itself may not always be an important one, but your performance in it is.

Mistakes

Learn from them. Write down the learning points if you like.

If you do that, then there is no need to give yourself a bad time over them. We all make mistakes, and always will; we don't need to tell ourselves how stupid we are for doing so.

*See **Let the good times roll***

Need

Most people respond much better to hearing that you 'need to' do something than if they hear that you 'would like to' or 'want to' do something.

This is particularly useful in the case where your access to a particular area is perhaps debatable. For example, 'I need to see the file on Smith' is much more likely to bring forth Smith's file than 'I would like to see the file on Smith.' Strange, but it's true.

Negotiating

You *must* learn to negotiate, even if you don't appear to be involved in formal negotiation. Much of life is to do with negotiation in either a formal or informal way, and it is a concept you should carry around with you.

Really, you should read a good book on negotiation, or go on a course, but just six tips:

- You negotiate on satisfaction, not money. For example, you may be willing to pay a bit extra to have an automatic garage door fitted if you think the firm will look after it if it goes wrong, will send a pleasant workman, etc. Money is *not* always the bottom line

- You can bring negotiation to deadlock, refuse to budge, come to a dead end. It shows how serious you are. Maybe the other person will come round, if not, then you can always re-open negotiation without losing face by going back with a suggestion of a minor amendment like, 'I've been thinking – supposing we made the door opening nine feet instead of ten feet; what could you do then?'

- Always keep it good natured. Even if you are at deadlock, avoid a quarrel – keep it good humoured.

- Just talk ordinarily to the person you're

negotiating with. When 'negotiating' don't use a special voice!

- Listen properly to what the other person is saying, and show that you've understood.
- Above all, when you're putting your own case, use only your best argument. **Your case is only as strong as the weakest argument you use to support it.**

Nervousness

Nervousness very rarely impresses people favourably even in the face of someone deliberately intimidating. You should therefore attempt to cover it up if you are able to.

Strangely, however, some people have cultivated it as a mannerism, usually in the hope they will put others at ease. This is a poor strategy, firstly because when you *do* have to be openly assertive it comes across as relatively 'heavy' and secondly because there are better ways of putting people at their ease, for example your **tone of voice** and non-verbal forms of communication.

Numeracy

There was a time, particularly in Britain, when the prime measure of a person's education and general sophistication was how literate and interested in literature that person was. Now, however, increasing emphasis is being put on numeracy – the ability to be at home with statistics, to do mental arithmetic quickly and easily, not to regard computers as in any way 'infra dig', and generally to accept that one can be both literate *and* numerate. Increasingly, it is not sufficient to be *either* literate or numerate, one must be both.

One at a time, please!

There are times when you are so busy that it is difficult to know what to do next, because it means not doing something else.

What most people do, wrongly, is to spend their time thinking how much there is to do and jumping from one thing to the next.

The real answer is to settle on one task. If it needs doing, do it. Do it as quickly, as pleasurably, and as well as you can, and then forget about it and get on to the next one. It is surprising how quickly the list gets shorter!

See *Clear the desk*

'One suggestion would be . . .'

A nice way of avoiding 'telling' and developing commitment instead. An example is:

'Given that we've left the notes behind, one suggestion would be that we ask the participants to hold a meeting to decide on the content of the two-day course.'

This encourages the listener to think about the question, and either to commit himself or put forward a more appropriate suggestion. Certainly, it engages the listener's mind, and gains their commitment, two vital objectives.

See **Brainstorming**

Ostrich imitations

If you know a problem exists, there is little to be gained from ignoring it unless you are pretty sure that it will cure itself of its own accord.

Parading one's ignorance

Some people make a point of being proud of their ignorance, for example, of:

- Computers
- Things mechanical
- Things electrical
- Anything to do with numbers
- Spelling.

There was once a time when it *was* slightly infra dig to be knowledgeable about the more tangible aspects of human life, but this is no longer so. The more things you know the better; if there are areas where you know you are *particularly* ignorant, then work to develop your knowledge in those areas. In the meantime, keep quiet about them.

Personal organizers

They are great. Make a point of finding out about them, find a system that suits you, and use it. It doesn't matter whether it's Filofax, time-manager, W.H.Smith or some electronic version. Find one that works for you.

There are lots of 'yuppie' jokes about organizers, but organized people stand a better chance than disorganized people.

There's not much to be said for being muddled!

Perfection

We all like to aim at perfection, but there comes a time when you have to ask yourself whether it is worthwhile. For example, which is better, to write one letter which is 99 per cent perfect, or to write four which are 95 per cent perfect in the same time?

Perfection is over-rated.

See **Fear of failure**

Persistence

Persistence is unequivocally an essential quality for a high flier. Certainly, it must be balanced with the ability to judge when one is being foolishly stubborn rather than admirably persistent, but, when in doubt, persist.

Perspective
(having a sense of)

The high flier must be able to maintain a balance between being enthusiastic about his or her work on the one hand, and having a realistic view about the relative importance of what he or she does in the overall scheme of things.

An example of failing to do this was the member of the British Diplomatic Service who referred to Hong Kong as being extremely important and South America as being a relative backwater. One could see why he said this. It is because the Diplomatic Service had been heavily involved in negotiating Hong Kong's future with China. However, it would be very difficult to make out a case that, in world terms, Hong Kong is really more important than South America.

To the outsider, it is difficult to see how the diplomat in the above example could possibly be so short-sighted. However, most people, in their own work, make similar mistakes from time to time.

Planning

As a general rule, people who plan do much better than those who don't.

See Goals

PR

Remember that 'public relations' is not only something that you do on behalf of your organization, it is also something you do for yourself.

What I mean is this. You should make sure that those who work with you know what you are good at. The best way to do this is simply to state, in the context of an appropriate conversation, 'I'm good at getting my work organized,' or 'I don't have trouble thinking of new ideas,' or whatever is *true* for you.

This last point, the truthfulness, is an important one. The listener has to recognize the truth of what you say, and register it.

On the whole, it is a valuable technique to be able to state, simply and modestly, even with humour if you like, what you are truly good at. You can tell people what they are good at too, if you like.

See **Compliments**

Preparation

Few people get away with a lack of preparation; no one benefits from being unprepared. In spite of this, most of us hope that we can 'get by' in situations by 'force of personality', 'native wit', 'using our charms', etc. So what situations must one prepare for? Most people with pretensions of being high fliers will have already grasped that there are some common situations, such as interviews and meetings where the real decisions may have already been taken before the group even assembles in the room. However, the need for preparation goes wider than this, and in reality means that any unfamiliar situation must be thought through before it is encountered. The essential skill here is being able to recognize when you are about to be in an unfamiliar situation.

Preparation, i.e., thinking through problems, need not be a long process; frequently even 30 seconds thought about a problem may prevent a *faux pas* or make subsequent progress substantially easier.

Priorities

Make the distinction between items which are *urgent*, and those which are *important*. The urgent ones need to be done first, the important ones may need more time spent on them.

Don't be ashamed of setting priorities, it needs to be done.

See Time management

Problem solving

A problem-solving approach to a crisis, or indeed any other problem is to:

- Identify the problem
- Brainstorm as many possible solutions as possible
- Assess the merits of each of the solutions
- Act on the preferred solution.

Easy, isn't it! Then why don't more managers use this technique? The most frequent difficulties are, firstly, to identify *exactly* what the problem is, and secondly, to brainstorm effectively. Many managers find difficulty in generating a large list of solutions – they cannot help but start to criticize a solution even before it is written down.

See **Brainstorming**

Procrastination

Don't do it.

Putting yourself forward

Some years ago, as a young psychologist in the Prison Department, I was at a meeting where the chairman wanted a videotape to be made of the work of prison psychologists. He wanted a subgroup to develop this idea and produce a 'draft' videotape.

This was something I very much liked the idea of, and it sounded like exciting stuff to me. For that reason I held back for a few moments but finally said that it was something I would like to be involved in. I can remember how one of my contemporaries looked surprised that I should volunteer in that way. But quickly two others had also volunteered, and we made a good show of it.

I would have kicked myself if I had let that opportunity go past, and I very nearly did. Curious how the very appeal of something can make you feel you should hold back from getting involved!

Relaxation

Learn to relax properly. There are various techniques, but two broad classifications are those which rely on you learning to relax different muscle groups in turn, and those which are based on meditation. Crucial to both is a calm relaxed breathing style. You don't need to attend evening classes, a good book or cassette tape will do very well. You *will* need to practise conscientiously, however – keep at it, it will be worthwhile.

'Rightly or wrongly...'

A useful little phrase to pre-empt criticism. An example is:

'Rightly or wrongly, what I did was to order 5,000 of these forms, even though they are very expensive.'

The implication of the 'rightly or wrongly' part is that, without saying so openly, you were aware that there were arguments for and against the decision, you weighed them up carefully, and came to a considered, correct decision. The overall effect is that the listener is reluctant to jump in with an over-hasty criticism of what is, evidently, a considered decision. An effect out of all proportion to how long it takes to say three words.

Saying 'No'

Sooner or later you have to learn to say 'No' Otherwise you are going to get very overloaded. This is how you do it:

1. Listen fully to what you are being asked to do.
2. Make a judgement as to whether you can do the task, taking into account your other commitments. If you can't, then . . .
3. Say you can't, clearly and unambiguously. But graciously, and maybe suggesting an alternative person for the task. Be clear that you cannot do it, but not brusque.
4. Terminate the discussion, either by changing the subject, or by physically leaving.
5. Sort out any guilt you have! You can only do so much.
6. In the unlikely event of you changing your mind, and deciding that you can do the task after all, get back to the person concerned.

It's easy really . . . just takes practice!

Secretaries

Other people's secretaries are a wonderful source of information, as they have access to everything, yet often do not know what is meant to be 'censored'; some are more than eager to demonstrate just how much information they are trusted with. For example, one secretary for a furniture removal company in conversation with a client who had had some furniture damaged during a removal, carefully explained how the boss usually tried to worm his way out of claims on his insurance because it meant that his premium went up next time.

So there are two key points to remember: the first is that it is worth chatting to other people's secretaries as a matter of course, so that you are in a good position to obtain information that otherwise might be difficult to get hold of; the second is to trust your own secretary a little bit more, so that he or she knows what information is to be censored, and why.

Self-congratulation

. . . is wonderful; it is what keeps you going. Beware of two things: make sure it is accurate and justified; do not forget **self-criticism** when that is justified.

Self-criticism

. . . is a necessary, if painful, part of one's development, made unnecessarily agonizing by some of its practitioners. Its purpose is to spot areas of one's performance that are weak, identify the weaknesses in simple tangible terms, and work on these weaknesses so that we perform better next time. Self-criticism is *not* meant to be a penance, a punishment or anything that makes you feel unnecessarily miserable; it is an objective process that leads on to better things next time.

See **Self-congratulation**

Self-efficacy

This is one of the few jargon terms you will find in this book, included because of its far reaching effectiveness and because there is really no Plain English translation for it.

The idea is a simple one. Those who can maintain an image of themselves as talented and effective turn out that way more often than those who don't. So it is important to nurture yourself, encourage yourself and keep yourself going well.

There are two techniques for achieving this: the first is to look back over the recent past regularly, highlight for yourself your main achievements, and give yourself a pat on the back. The other is just a shade more tricky: it is to imagine yourself delivering an impeccable performance in your job, imagine just what it entails, and yourself doing it. It can be fun!

*See **Let the good times roll***

Self-examination

At one hospital where I worked there was a consultant psychiatrist who was new to the ward he was to be responsible for. In truth, he was a shy chap who came across as being somewhat aloof, disdainful and stand-offish. Needless to say, this did not sit very well with the nursing staff, some of whom proceeded to give him a pretty bad time.

He could have reacted to this simply by becoming upset and introverted, but instead, he set about examining his own performance and the total situation. Gradually, he was able to work on making reasonable relationships with key members of the nursing staff and slowly became properly integrated into the ward.

There are plenty of other examples where a logical appraisal of the situation, unafraid to recognize your own weaknesses (and strengths), pays huge dividends. Much better than a simple emotional reaction or burying your head in the sand.

Keep a running two column list if you like; one column for your strengths, one for your weaknesses. Make the first column longer!

See **Diary**

Setting your own standards

Just because your boss has not chased you about the task he asked you to do a week ago, it does not mean that everything is all right. If you know it should have been done by now, get it done!

Sexism, racism, 'age-ism', etc.

. . . are nonsense. If you think you need the help of blind prejudice to get on in the world, then give up now.

Shutting up

One of the commonest criticisms of others is that they 'don't know when to shut up'. This is not simply that, by going on, they become tedious or boring; more than that, they either get themselves into deep water by saying something that they would have been better off not saying or that they simply weakened the impact they would have had if they had stopped at the right time.

We have all experienced the feeling of not knowing how to finish off what we're saying at the right moment. Nine times out of ten it is no problem; we simply say what we have to say and that is that. Other times, we know that we would be best off stopping now, but . . . !

Some people demonstrate a repertoire of good short phrases for stopping what they're saying at the right point. Phrases such as: 'I think I'll leave it at that,' or 'No, I'll stop there,' or even 'Period' (horrible word) or 'Full-stop' (which is as nearly as bad!) are all useful little phrases, if you remember to use them.

Simplicity

Keep it simple. No matter what 'it' is, just keep it simple.

Start with 'A's not with 'C's

You know what the 'A' tasks are: they're the important ones, the ones that will help you get where you're going.

You also know what your 'C' tasks are: they're the niggly little things that don't matter too much whether you do them or not. They're also the ones that many people 'clear out of the way' before getting down to the real work.

The problem is that you can spend so much time clearing 'C' tasks out of the way that you have no time left to do the really important ones – the 'A' tasks.

Launch right in and get on with the 'A' tasks; do a few 'C's, if you have time, later.

See Priorities

77

The streetwise versus the diplomat

Some bosses get on really quickly by being streetwise, assertive and blunt. They get near the top of their organization, and then find those qualities aren't enough. Their shortage of tact, perception and diplomacy lets them down and they either go no further or even come badly unstuck. Equally there are plenty of sensitive and diplomatic people who never get anywhere.

Both qualities are necessary – you have to balance energy, drive and worldliness with the ability to understand others, to smooth their feathers and to get the best out of them. A tricky balancing act!

CHAIRMAN

Taking your opportunities

I was once employed to offer advice to a leading football club manager. The post of manager for the national side was looking as though it would shortly be vacant, and he felt it would be offered to him.

His one worry was that it was going to be offered to him 'for the wrong reasons'. Something to do with the unavailability of another possible candidate. This made him say that he would decline the post, if indeed he was offered it.

I was (almost!) speechless, for once. However I did manage to convince him not to be quite so falsely principled.

We should all do our level best to progress our careers. But, if a bit of luck comes your way, take it with both hands.

(There was a happy ending to this particular tale!)

The 'to do' list

Make out a list each morning which tells you what you are aiming to achieve that day. That sounds easy enough, doesn't it? Then why is it that people don't do it, or that it doesn't work when they try to do it? Three reasons:

- The list has to be manageable. You have to recognize that reactive tasks will crop up and allow time for them in planning your 'active' tasks. Just because you don't know in advance what the interruptions will be does not mean you shouldn't budget time for them
- The list should consist of 'A' tasks; not 'C's
- Completing the list should give you a sense of achievement. This means you go home brighter and more fulfilled.

The telephone

Use it a lot – it pays off!
  (If you really want to read some more, then three factors are:

- Compared with letters, it opens up communication so that you make available to yourself all manner of new information
- Compared with meeting someone face to face it may not be quite so good, but one frequently either doesn't have time or doesn't 'bother' to see others face to face. You usually can bother to pick the telephone up
- In persuading people to do what they would rather not, the telephone is much better than writing, though not as good as a face to face meeting.

There are others, but it is all said in the very first sentence!)

Thinking

In a survey of psychologists in one government department, where the 80 people surveyed were asked to keep a detailed record of their work for two weeks, only one person listed 'thinking' as an activity that he indulged in. This may simply have been an oversight on the part of the other respondents, but it may not. Many people fail to achieve their potential simply because they do not make any attempt to think coherently.

See **Energy**

Time keeping

Once out of fashion for high fliers – it was felt that a truly busy and important person could not possibly arrive at a meeting, for example, bang on time; it would suggest that he or she had previously been sitting doing nothing, waiting for it.

Now, thankfully, and correctly, many more people are seeing lateness as more a sign of bad organization than of being busy. Always be punctual if you can.

Time management

In Britain there tends to be a degree of scepticism about time management and its associated efficiency. There should be no debate: good time management is better than bad time management. There are several rules for good time management.

- Regularly make a list of your goals, short-and long-term, work and personal
- Put your goals in order of priority
- Make a list of things you need to do to achieve these goals
- Every day, make a list of things you will achieve that day.

Threatened?
Don't be!

Many people feel 'threatened', that is, they feel under potential criticism even if reality doesn't bear this out, especially in meetings and when talking to superiors.

Try not to be; be as open, bold and straightforward as you can. If you make errors, you can put them right at a later date; if you are too quiet, defensive and timid, that is difficult ever to put right.

Tone of voice

Try to develop a warm tone of voice, because with that you can say things that would otherwise be too 'heavy'.

Research shows that in everyday conversations, people normally forget the actual words that were spoken after a few days or weeks, and are simply left with the tone of the conversation – friendly, aggressive, interesting, boring, etc.

In business, people remember more of the words spoken, because of their importance. However, the tone of voice is still vital, as for example, when giving criticism. By using a neutral or warm tone to deliver the critical comments, one can give the otherwise difficult message that you think the individual is a fine person, but it is just this particular act that needs closer examination, thereby making the important distinction between an individual and his actions.

Unidimensionality

Unidimensionality – here meaning the wish to see things in one dimension, the wish to find one simple solution to a problem – is the universal characteristic of a low flier. Low fliers therefore pose questions such as 'What is the answer to criminality? Is it to introduce harsher sentences? No? Then what is it?'

High fliers are prone to, and enjoy, seeing things in a more realistic (and, unfortunately, usually more complicated) way. Therefore, in this example, they may suggest that criminality might be reduced by:

- Training parents to bring up their children better
- Strengthening the police force
- Ensuring most laws are recognized as fair and just by all of the population. (And many others.)

To a low flier such an analysis is simply tedious and boring. However, this is encouraging to a true high flier, as it is one of the characteristics that is most difficult to imitate.

Urgency and importance

Successful people spend the best part of their time doing important tasks. Less successful people get bogged down in urgent tasks which are not necessarily important. These are the people who, at a certain age, look back at their lives and ask where it has disappeared to, and why they have nothing substantial to show for it.

Do urgent tasks straight away, but don't spend much time on them unless they are important as well. Your important tasks are those which help you achieve your goals. Make sure you know what these tasks are, and spend the bulk of your time on them.

See Goals and Reactive tasks

Voice

Like your appearance, your voice quality creates just as big an impression as the ideas which you put forward, and you can work on the quality of your voice.

Voice training is outside the scope of this book, but here is a list of some attributes of voice quality which you can think about and work on if you choose to:

- *Pitch* High-pitched or deep or somewhere between
- *Tone of voice* For example, friendly, aggressive, blunt, approachable, uncertain, open and so on
- *Speed* How quickly or slowly you speak. Most people with 'interesting' voices actually vary the speed at which they speak; they don't speak at a constant speed
- *Volume* How loud or softly one speaks. Like speed it is good to vary this
- *Accent* Some regional accents are much more acceptable than others, and whether you should try to change your accent is your personal decision.

What to do and how to do it

First, decide what you want to do, then decide how to do it. It sounds straightforward, and it is. Why is it then that so many people contaminate their decisions by worrying about questions of feasibility?

The correct process is to decide what you are trying to achieve, and *then* how to achieve it. If it really *is* impossible, then go back to a different option. In reality, you can nearly always achieve your preferred option, so why go for anything else?

Your strengths and weaknesses

This one is easy:

- You should know (have a written list of) what your strengths are, and consciously play to them – utilize them to the full
- You should know equally well what your weaknesses are and,
  - (a) try to develop in those areas
  - (b) try to avoid situations which crucially expose your weaknesses
  - (c) try to get 'cover' (for example by asking someone for advice) in situations where you are weak.

See **Self-examination**

Turbulence and Dogfights

Sometimes things don't go smoothly: rivals try to put you down along the way, or else you hit a bumpy patch that needs skilful handling. These phrases and observations are of relevance mainly to these times.

'Balls' 93

The bottom line . . .
   saying it 94

Broken record 95

Calling foul 96

Can I remind you about . . . ?
   97

Disparaging, devaluing,
   decrying 97

Eye-contact (or looking at
   someone) 98

'For obvious reasons . . .' 99

Hares and hounds 100

'I don't know how' 101

If you want them to read it . . .
   102

Inuendoes and implications
   103

Irritations 104

'I shouldn't say this, but . . .'
   105

'I think this is a serious matter'
   106

'It's as you were saying
   earlier . . .' 107

'It stands to reason . . .' 107

'I've actually thought about
   this over several years' 108

Losing your temper 109

'My dear' 110

'No' 111

Non-verbal communication
   112

'Pardon?' 113

Phone calls, letters and
   visits 114

Plain English 115
Pressure 116
Problems are better than
    solutions 117
Put-downs 117
Questions you don't want to
    answer 119
Relationships 120
Sex 120
Simplistic 121
Taking things personally 122
'Thank you' 123
That's not your previous
    story' 124

'There are two ways of looking
    at this' 125
'To be fair to Fred . . .' 126
Turning crises into
    opportunities 127
'We' 128
'What Angela says is quite
    correct' 129
When you're tired and
    down 130
Your place or mine? 131
'You've already admitted
    that . . .' 132

'Balls'

An example of a word whose most common usage is to indicate disagreement with another person's argument!

The beauty of such words is that you do not need to get involved in any form of logical response to a well-argued case. The reason for this may be that you think the other's case is such nonsense that only an expletive will do, or alternatively, that it is so sound that you would be on to a loser trying to argue against it rationally!

The bottom line
... saying it

How do we best go about telling someone the price of an expensive item? Equally, how do we best state our strong, 'bottom line' opinions?

The answer is that we should state them clearly, but soften the blow a little by carrying on talking.

So, instead of saying, 'This costs £10,000,' we say, 'This costs £10,000, which includes a pre-delivery inspection, delivery, insurance and any other expenses incurred along the way.' That way, we give the recipient a little time to regain his or her composure after hearing the price, and, perhaps more important, feel easier ourselves about 'the bottom line'.

The same applies to 'bottom line opinions'. If one wishes to say, 'I think what you did was quite wrong,' one should in fact say, 'I think what you did was quite wrong because . . .' Either way is equally strong, but by carrying on talking you soften the blow a little and stand a greater chance of continuing a useful conversation.

Broken record

This is a useful technique borrowed from assertiveness training. The idea is that you state your point of view (which may be contentious) repeatedly if necessary, without being deflected by arguments the other person puts forward – just like a record with a nick on it keeps repeating the same line.

For example:

'I felt very offended when you became angry towards me in yesterday's meeting, and I would prefer you didn't behave that way again.'

'Yes, but what you had said was completely incorrect and was misleading the others.'

'I'm just saying that I was very offended by you becoming angry in that way and would prefer it didn't happen again.'

And so on, *ad nauseam*.

The advantage of this is that it is highly assertive yet polite, so can be used equally with subordinates or superiors.

Calling foul

This is a technique used at meetings. Sometimes, a person with an opposing point of view to yours will go a bit over the top in what they say. It's important to spot this immediately and call foul.

How do you do this? Simply by using a strong phrase which registers your offence . . . 'I think that's a disgraceful thing to say' or something similar. It's a difficult one for your opponent to get back from. They will be embarrassed, and their whole argument will seem as unreasonable as the over-the-top statement that you have highlighted.

Curiously, though, many such O.T.T. statements seem simply strong and powerful unless you call foul in this way. Some people get away with whatever you will let them!

Can I remind you about . . . ?

Simply a polite and more acceptable form of 'Knowing you, you probably won't know about . . .'

Disparaging, devaluing, decrying

Running down others' views is very rarely a good idea, no matter how much you disagree with them. Disagree certainly, put your own point of view as strongly as you wish, but don't sneer.

Eye-contact (or looking at someone)

There is lots to know about eye-to-eye contact, but just two pieces of information will suffice quite nicely for our purposes.

- Eye-to-eye contact exaggerates whatever emotion is taking place at the time in question. So, if you are in a friendly, intimate situation, eye contact enhances that intimacy; if you are in an argument, eye-contact will exaggerate the hostility and, therefore, might be best avoided
- Those in a subordinate position tend to look at their superior more than vice versa. This can be important in deciding the pecking order in an apparently equal group, but it is of course only one factor.

'For obvious reasons . . .'

This is a rather risky phrase. Its usual use is, for example, 'The first plan is unworkable, for obvious reasons.' Usually, in a statement like this, the first plan is not actually unworkable. Whether or not you get away with it depends on the sophistication of the audience. If the people in the audience are slightly unsure of themselves, they may not risk challenging you. However, it only takes one confident person to say, politely, but devastatingly, 'I'm sorry, but I am afraid the reasons are not at all obvious to me. I wonder if you could explain why you think the first plan is unworkable?' to put you in a very tight spot. It may be difficult to retrieve the situation.

A phrase that is probably best avoided.

Hares and hounds

You *can* run with both the hare and the hounds.
More than that – you *should* do so.

Tradition says that you can't be in two rival
camps at the same time, but this assumes that
your work relationships are based on personalities
and personal considerations. In your working life,
this should not be so; you are working to do the
best for your organization, largely regardless of
personality and other considerations. Try to keep
out of the personality conflicts which afflict all
organizations, and let everyone respect you for
your clear commitment to the organization
regardless of other considerations. Remember
though, you are aiming to be gentle to both parties,
not to offend both (which is easily done!).

'I don't know'

Another phrase which you need to be able to say, and which is much better than bluffing. There is no need to take a pride in saying it at every opportunity, however. Some folk do this, assuming, perhaps, that they will be admired for their gutsy, down-to-earth honesty. They are not, of course.

There are numerous euphemisms for 'I don't know'. 'I'll have to get back to you on that one,' and 'I'll need advance notice of that,' are two good ones.

If you want them to read it . . .

There are a number of rules about writing documents (even memos and such) so that people are inclined to read them. Here are some:

1. Lower case letters are easier to read than upper case. Therefore, reserve upper case for short sequences such as headlines.
2. A typeface with serifs (the twiddly bits) is easier to read than a sans-serif typeface. Reserve sans-serif for headlines.
3. Have between 36 and 72 characters per line. Over 72 makes life very difficult for the reader. With modern, proportionally-spacing word processors this is an easy error to fall foul of.
4. On a two-or-more page document, try to ensure that the page endings don't coincide with sentence endings. People usually want to finish a sentence . . . you can use that fact to entice them to turn over the page.

Innuendoes and implications

Don't be over-sensitive or defensive, but there are times when you are pretty sure that your performance is being criticized, not openly, but by implication, innuendo or hints. How do you handle it?

The answer, of course, depends upon whether your performance warrants criticism. Let us assume that, because you are brilliant, conscientious and hard working, you do not deserve this condemnation; what do you do?

The answer is that you confront it. Not angrily, not necessarily even in an annoyed way, but confront it nevertheless. You say something along the lines of, 'It sounds as though you are implying that . . .' or 'I feel as though I'm being criticized here, because there is an implication that . . .'

At this, your potential adversary should back down. (Remember we are assuming your performance is not actually open to criticism!) Assuming he or she does, then you should also register it in the minds of any others who are present with a fairly definite 'Good' or the softer 'I'm very pleased to hear you make that clear,' or your own words along those lines. If your adversary doesn't back down, then it should be easy for you to put them down (remember you're in the clear).

But what if your performance really was below par? In that case, the safest option is simply to consider yourself lucky that the criticism is merely by implication or innuendo. Keep quiet!

Irritations

Get rid of 'irritating' tasks as quickly as you can. The longer they linger at the back of your mind, the longer they sap your optimism, and it is optimism you need to produce constructive ideas and energetic work performance.

Don't curse the fact that irritating, annoying tasks are part of your life – they are part of life for everyone. Just do them straight away, and get on with something better. Be aware of what is 'playing on your mind' and get it off, quickly!

'I shouldn't say this, but...'

If you shouldn't say it, then don't. No one will be impressed by the air of confidentiality that you are attempting to impart.

'I think this is a serious matter'

This phrase is used when someone in a group has just made a little quip about a statement you have made, and thereby made it look ridiculous. This can be particularly irritating, because it effectively closes discussion on the topic, without the other person having put forward a sensible alternative view.

'I think this is a serious matter,' said reasonably lightly, gives people a mild attack of conscience and gets them ready to hear more. The phrase must be followed quickly by a phrase such as, 'I think we should examine the pros and cons of the plan I put forward carefully, or any better alternatives if anyone can suggest some.'

'It's as you were saying earlier . . .'

A useful little phrase to gain someone's attention. People always prick up their ears to hear repeated something that they have said. In reality, what you say does not have to be exactly what was said earlier!

'It stands to reason . . .'

This refers to a 'fact' for which there is no evidence. Beware of it.

See **Commonsense**

'I've actually thought about this over several years'

Used mischievously in reply to another person's argument, opinion or statement.

The key bit is 'I've actually thought about this'; the 'over several years/months/weeks' part simply softens it so that the recipient cannot call 'foul'. The function of the whole sentence is, of course, to imply that the other person hasn't thought about it at all. However, since that is not actually stated, how can they object?

Losing your temper

Never a good idea.
   Certainly, it makes an impact on people, but it has two crucial drawbacks:

* You run the risk of discouraging your colleagues from telling you things in future. In other words, you have simply altered what they say rather than what they do
* You run the risk of giving your subordinates the impression that you are angry with them as people, rather than what they have done in that specific instance. This will demoralize and lead to a breakdown in your **relationships**.

*See **Compliance and acceptance***

'My dear'

This is a condescending put-down used by a man to a woman, usually a young one. No self-respecting man would even think of using it, but women should know how to respond.

Probably the best response is to act like you didn't hear it. The 'My dear' put-down is only made effective by the woman recipient becoming cross or petulant, because that is subsequently hinted at being 'typical of women'.

So, ignore it if you wish. However, some women are adept at keeping their cool and replying sensibly to whatever is the topic of debate but suffixing their reply with a wryly humorous '. . . my sweet' or other term of mock endearment.

Whatever you do, though, *don't* lose your cool; it's doing that which makes the put-down work.

'No'

Learn to say this word, because it enables you to turn down what other people are trying to put on to you, and decide for yourself which direction you want to go in.

It needs practice to be able to say it without causing offence.

Non-verbal communication

Extremely useful, sometimes even more useful than the verbal sort. The advantage of it is that you can communicate things that you would otherwise be reluctant to say, and no one can criticize you for it. For example in a meeting you can communicate non-verbally:

'I'm fed up with this.'
'Can't we go on to the next item?'
'Doesn't he go on!'
'Whenever is this going to end?'

You can also express positive feelings, like:

'Spot on, mate.'
'Keep it up.'

All done with sighs, raised eyebrows, shuffling, looking out of the window, smiling, winking. Be careful with the last of these!

'Pardon?'

Pardon is, of course, used where you have not heard something that has been said to you. There is, however, a more deliberate use, in response to a particularly vitriolic challenge.

For example, if you are on the receiving end of, 'Do you not think that the statement you have just made is typical of the kind of person who has spent all his life in an ivory tower and is not in touch with those on the ground floor where all the action happens?' said in a strident and challenging tone.

One possible response to this is, 'Pardon – I am sorry I missed some of that.' It is very difficult, if not impossible, for your challenger to repeat his statement with the same forcefulness, and even if they suspect that you really had heard what they said, there is very little that they can do.

Alternative responses are, 'Quite possibly,' (this technique known as 'fogging' – making a response that is not substantial enough for the others to get their hands on), or 'No,' which usually brings a laugh from any others present.

Phone calls, letters and visits

If you want to persuade someone to do something for you, and it's touch and go whether that individual will agree, the most effective way is to go round and see him or her face to face.

The second most effective way is to call them on the telephone.

The least likely to succeed is a letter.

Plain English

In principle, Plain English is excellent. True high fliers will express first rate ideas clearly in plain, straightforward English that can be easily understood by the person who reads or hears it.

If you are not sure of the quality of your ideas though, or if you are not sure if you are a real high flier, then be wary of plain English – simple ideas in simple English can easily create the impression that the piece has been written by a juvenile.

For example, if you say, 'More resources will be needed to do this job properly,' 'resources' may mean money, temporary secretarial support, the loan of a mechanical digger, or almost anything else.

Whatever it is, say it plainly; this helps others' thinking as well as your own.

Pressure

Pressure, like beauty, is largely in the eye of the beholder. Certainly some people have more pressured lives than others, but it is the way we react to it that is important. Keep **relaxed** and cope with the situations that befall you without resorting to winding yourself up with mutterings about the unnecessary **interruptions** and niggles that happen to you. If it all gets too much, stop and relax properly. Do not allow yourself to get 'bogged down'. Above all, don't wind yourself up – plenty of others will do that for you.

Problems are better than solutions!

There are a few times when this is true, and the main occasion is when you want to persuade someone to do what you want. A straightforward request often elicits the 'I would, but . . .' response; sometimes a statement of the problem works better because it leaves the listener with the joy of producing the solution (and acting on it).

For example, a (real) nurse said to a patient just about to go in to see the doctor, 'Don't say you want painkillers or that will be the last thing you get – just tell him you've got a headache.'

The same principle works on a much greater scale too. Maybe you've tried it. If not, give it a go.

Put-downs

Put-downs are usually best avoided, although it is important to be able to deliver one if needs be. The most frequent scenario for appropriate put-downs is during meetings. This is because one's credibility is at stake, as one's performance is open to 'public scrutiny' and comparison with the performance of others.

Therefore, what one aims to do in a meeting is to be good to those who are good to you and give a bad time to those who are bad to you. Simple, but many people are good at rewarding *or* punishing, but not both.

Where the 'put-down' comes in is that it *is* the appropriate response to those who give you a bad time. Only use it as a last resort; people respect neither those who are *forever* putting others down nor those who are *incapable* of putting others down.

How do you do it? You watch others, and learn from them, but there are a few general rules:

• Put downs are usually short, not long-winded
• They are delivered in a pointed tone, but not in an angry, irate or annoyed one
• They may rely on sarcasm, pointing out an error in logic, or omission of fact
• They may rely on putting in derogatory information about the victim's work performance
• They do not have to be delivered immediately, although it is best if you can think quickly enough.

So, use put-downs on the rare occasions when they really are appropriate, but remember, too, to boost people when they are good to you.

See **Compliments** *and* **'We'**

Questions you don't want to answer

There are generally two reasons for not wanting to answer a question:

- You do not want to divulge the information that is being asked for
- Where someone, usually in a group, has asked a question deliberately to put you on the spot, rather than necessarily to obtain information.

Coping with the first case simply involves accepting the idea that you don't have to reply to particular questions that are posed to you. In practice, this means that you answer another, imaginary question. Politicians are adept at doing this.

In the second case, to avoid being put on the spot and apparently justifying oneself, the most useful phrase is frequently, 'Why do you ask that?' This can be said perfectly amicably, but it effectively turns the tables. There are an infinite number of ways of rephrasing 'Why do you ask that?' if the question is later repeated to you.

Relationships

At a high level most things are done through relationships – the good offices that one has with others. Very rarely can one *insist* on having one's own way and come out on top in the long run. You can be blocked by too many people at too many hurdles, and those who do not realize this cut out a very difficult life for themselves. This is taken to the extreme by the European head of a multi-national car company who keeps files on almost everyone he meets, so that, for example, he can call into virtually any large dealership that he has visited before and ask after the manager's wife and children by name.

See **Compliance versus acceptance**

Sex

People don't like to hear about you having sex with anybody except your spouse. If they do, they will use it against you.

Particularly, never have sex with a subordinate. No good will come of it!

Simplistic

The word 'simplistic' is a put-down, and a devastating one, because, if you are on the receiving end of it, it implies that what you have said is simple, meaning stupid.

If you are the recipient of the accusation, the best response is: 'Why do you think that is simplistic?' This almost invariably leads to a stumbling response and ultimately a banal apology for a reason.

You are probably best off avoiding antagonistic phrases such as 'simplistic', but, if you must use them, then make sure that you carry straight on with your own views, so that your rival cannot get in with the crushing, but deceptively polite, 'In what way?' response.

See **Intelligence**

Taking things personally

Don't. The time for taking things personally is in one's personal life.

In professional life one should, needless to say, take things professionally. This means taking criticism and dealing with it by examining whether there are learning points for similar situations in the future.

Taking things personally not only builds up **stress** but also, paradoxically, puts one's essential **relationships** at risk.

'Thank you'

The 'hidden' use for 'thank you' is to ensure that others realize that it is *you* who deserves the credit (if you do!).

Imagine this scene:

> You have convened a selection panel to interview job applicants, and the selection goes smoothly. Frequently those involved do not know exactly how the panel came into being or exactly who was responsible for it, and one member says at the end of the procedure, 'Well, that all seemed to go very smoothly and well.'

You can hardly then say, 'Only because I organized it like that. You do realize that it was *me* who organized it, don't you?' But you *can* say, 'Thank you', which carries exactly the same message.

'That's not your previous story'

in conjunction with

'Yes, but you've used that argument before'

A slightly dubious pair of phrases, for use when you are belaboured with someone's repeated arguments.

You are bound to be able to use one or other of these phrases, and either one is sufficient to turn the tables long enough to give you breathing space!

'There are two ways of looking at this'

A gentle way of introducing a controversial idea. It thereby forestalls its immediate rejection.

The way it works is to say: 'There are two ways of looking at this. The first is . . .' here you say the conventional way. You then go on with 'The other way would be . . .' introducing a more controversial perspective. Step three is to open up discussion by listing some of the pros and cons of each. You have now achieved your goal, serious consideration is being given to an idea which would have been too contentious if launched 'from cold'.

'To be fair to Fred...'

This phrase can be used in two ways:

- Introducing your defence of Fred, replying to others' attack on him
- A below-the-belt phrase in response to criticism of a project that you appear to have been responsible for, making it plain (rightly or wrongly) that it was not really you who was responsible, but poor old Fred. Better used when Fred isn't there, but, even if he is, it sounds as though you are being eminently reasonable.

Turning crises into opportunities

'Crises' can be defined as 'something unexpected happening to thwart your plans'. There are two ways of reacting to this: one is to curse your bad fortune, or, worse still, to curse others' incompetence; the other is to view the situation as one which *forces* you to review your plans, and, by thinking creatively, maybe spot an opportunity in a new direction, that you had not thought of.

Therefore, in crises, always try to continue thinking optimistically; certainly you may have to restructure your plans, but, who knows, this enforced constructive thinking may produce an even better opportunity than the original plan.

See **Brainstorming**

'We'

'We' is a wonderful word that carries with it a meaning out of all proportion to its size. Saying 'We' when you really mean 'I' (the royal 'we') is a slightly pompous and irritating habit, but using it appropriately can generate a great feeling of goodwill and co-operation.

A man who had hijacked a bus with 23 passengers on board and forced one of them to drive the bus in a getaway attempt, was asked why he felt so well disposed to the unwilling driver. (One of the few white men on the bus he did not either kill or wound). His reply included the fact that the hostage/driver constantly referred to the two of them as 'we', as in, 'We ain't ever gonna get away with this,' a phrase which implied a goodwill towards the perpetrator that could never have been stated outright.

That then, is the main strength of 'we'; it can imply a togetherness and feeling of co-operation that can never be stated outright. Avoid 'we' if you really mean 'I'.

'What Angela says is quite correct'

This is the phrase to use if you want to be one up on Angela (or Fred, or whoever). It nicely implies that you are the *real* expert, whereas Angela is merely playing at it.

But on the other hand, how can Angela object? On the face of it you are simply agreeing with her and backing her up.

When you're tired and down

Everyone, but everyone, gets tired; everyone has times when they are 'down'. There is nothing wrong with that, and, if you must work during these times, there are probably plenty of routine tasks that you can do.

What you must *not* do, however, is to make important decisions, or do any vital actions. This can be much more difficult than it seems, as sometimes important events do happen when you are simply not on top form. Try to postpone them if you can; they may well be important, but are they really *that* urgent? If something *is* important, then do it when you are at your best; even a crisis can often be confronted after a good night's sleep.

See Urgency and importance

Your place or mine?

It is important whose office you use when you meet with a colleague. If you go to their office, this implies that they have a higher status than you, and vice versa. On the other hand, if you are in a rush, it is much easier to leave someone else's office to get on with your work than it is to get them to leave yours.

So, if your priority is status, try to get them round to your place. But, if you want to keep the conversation short, go round to theirs, and leave when you want!

'You've already admitted that...'

An unfair phrase which puts down another person's argument without recourse to any logical reasoning.

An example:

Scene: Two opposing politicians discussing a government scheme.

Politician 1: Grandly describes government commitment to solving the problem, how carefully the solution has been contrived, and how the magnificent sum of £10m has been allocated.

Politician 2: 'You've already admitted that this scheme will cost £10m and I believe there are many other priorities we should be addressing.'

It is the word 'admitted' that casts a blight on what his opponent has said, without any good reasoning. The basic ploy is, of course, the word 'admitted', added to something one's opponent has actually said. It is then difficult for them to wrangle their way out of it!

See **'Balls'**

Cruising

So you have reached your required altitude, but can you stay there? More to the point, can you stay there easily, without undue strain on you or those around you? Are you still looking to develop yourself, and make life easier for you, your colleagues and subordinates? Here are some concepts which should help.

All things to all men 135

Alphabetical order 135

Always brief the team together 136

Ambiguity 137

Annual reports, appraisal interviews and so on 138

Assertiveness 138

Bad news 139

Big decisions, small decisions 139

Blaming others 140

Boat-burning 140

Boorish behaviour — phrases to excuse it 141

Bullet-proof 142

A 'businesslike attitude' 142

The car 143

Chairing 144

Checking 145

Choice 146

Commonsense 147

Compliane versus acceptance 148

Computer games, juggling and cricket 149

Consulting 150

Contaminating the decision 151

Counter control 152

A day's work 153

Delegation 154

Democratic decision making 155

Diary 156

Diffusion of responsibility 157

Don't phrase things negatively (!) 158

Do the worst tasks first 159

Executive toys 160

Exercise 161

Expert 162

Fear of failure 163

Fudging 164

Fun 165

Gut reaction 165

Holidays — the five basic rules 166

Indecision 167

An individual and his actions 168

Interruptions 169

'I told them how to do it' 170

Job interviews — phrases people use to describe themselves 171

Keeping your options open 171

Key questions 172

Lack of co-operation 173

Laws of physics 174

Leadership 175

Letters, typing and presentation 176

Luck 177

Manner 177

Modesty 178

Must 179

Names — forgetting them 180

Note-taking 181

Optimism 182

Pacing 182

Paperwork 183

Partners 183

Personnel selection 185

Persuasion 186

Playing to your strengths 187

The posh office 188

Positive and negative control 189

Power 190

Pressure interviews 191

Protest 192

Putting it in writing 193

Quiet time 194

Reactive tasks 195

Reserved spaces in the car park 196

Risky shift 197

Scoundrels and vagabonds 198

Secretaries — getting on with them 199

'Seeking a fresh challenge' 200

Self-esteem 201

Setting limits 202

Shoes 203

Silence 204

Sleeping on it 205

Solemn and serious 206

Stress 207

Threats 209

Training films/books 210

Trust your staff 211

Voting 211

Walking the job 212

Work is more fun than fun 213

All things to all men

This, you cannot be. You have to decide your style so stick to it. You might choose to be an easy-going, friendly individual; you might choose to be an aggressive, dynamic, thrusting person, or one of the shades in between these two.

Two rules to bear in mind when you are deciding:

- You must have an image which can be conveyed in a few words, as in the examples above
- Your image must be in line with, and close to, your natural personality, otherwise the strain will become apparent both to others and to yourself.

Alphabetical order

Always use it, for example, on distribution lists and so on. You will avoid more offence than you'd ever believe.

Always brief the team together

The conventional reason for this is that any inconsistencies in the instructions you give come to light and are resolved before becoming problematical.

Further than that though, it means that you have to avoid fudging issues. I recall being one of a group of consultants discussing what the hospital head had said to us individually. Inevitably, different things had been said to each of us. Maybe it was our faulty recollections of the conversation, maybe he really had said different things to each of us. Who knows. Either way, if he had spoken to us en masse he would have avoided all the evil things that were said of him when the apparent differences came to light. It's foolish to think that people don't talk to each other!

Ambiguity

Avoid ambiguity in documents, proposals and policy, especially if it is deliberate 'fudging' or 'sitting on the fence'.

At best it produces confusion, at worst it produces paranoia. If your subordinates are not clear what your proposals are, they will certainly assume bad news rather than good news! Even if you know the document will be received reluctantly, make sure its contents are clear as this also serves to clarify *your* thoughts; you know what you would fight for and what you wouldn't.

Annual reports, appraisal interviews and so on

At best, almost useless. At worst, misleading and destructive.

Sometimes the recipient is told that it is his or her opportunity to say what they think of their progress, or some such platitude. Of course it isn't.

Their real purpose is to make some manager feel that they are in control of the whole organization by having a load of reports.

Give them up!

Assertiveness

The ability to state your point of view, and usually to swing a decision in the direction that you want, without being aggressive, bullying or underhand.

A difficult quality to develop, but one which high fliers have.

Bad news

If you have bad news to give someone, give it to them before someone else does. If they hear it elsewhere, it will probably have been elaborated and it will certainly not be in the form in which you would have presented it. More importantly you will have lost a person's trust; if you were keeping that bit of news from him, (who's to know you really were going to tell him?), then what else are you hiding?

Big decisions, small decisions

The difference between a big decision and a small decision is reversibility. If a decision can be easily reversed, then it's a small decision, deserving a small amount of time. If it's difficult or impossible to reverse, then you had better think pretty carefully about it!

Blaming others

Not a particularly useful thing to do. It is of course possible to change others' behaviour, but not so easily as you might change your own. Therefore, a key question to ask yourself when others have done things that you would rather they hadn't, is, 'What could I have done, so that they would have behaved differently?'

Boat-burning

Usually projects start with an idea, then consideration of feasibility, then design and development, then advertising of the product.

It can take a long time, partly because there is often no real pressure on you to complete the project.

There are a *few* projects, however, where burning your boats can *usefully* put the pressure on you. Suppose, for example, you do things in reverse order and advertise the product first! It can get things done an awful lot quicker. Be careful, though, what you apply this to . . . advertising a one-week course, due to start in six months' time puts useful pressure on you to design and develop the course; on the other hand, advertising a transistor radio you have not yet had designed is a very poor idea!

Boorish behaviour – phrases to excuse it

- *'Life is unfair'* (The implication being that you too are entitled to be unfair; you are only running true to form – doing your duty almost.)
- *'It's not a perfect world'* (And therefore your imperfect decisions are to be expected. Probably even better than so-called perfect decisions.)

Don't use either of these phrases; don't imply either of the dreadful statements in brackets.

Bullet-proof

Some individuals believe they are invulnerable. This feeling comes from the status of their office, or the belief that they will be backed by influential people who support them.

In reality, everyone is responsible to someone; there is an area where each of us is vulnerable and there are plenty of people ready and willing to prove that this is so. Richard Nixon demonstrated this on a grand scale, but many humbler individuals continue to follow in his footsteps.

A 'businesslike attitude'

You don't need it. Being friendly and approachable does not mean that you are not also well-organised and energetic. Equally, being formal and slightly rushed (a businesslike attitude?) need not suggest productivity.

The car

In partnerships, cars cause more trouble than just about everything else put together.

Think seriously about leaving each partner to sort out their own car, privately, not through the partnership. If you insist on arranging the cars through the firm, then you had better make very sure you have a watertight system for them.

What is that system? I don't know. And neither, it seems, does anyone else.

Chairing

When chairing a meeting, remember how best to handle the discussion on problems that require solutions:

- Introduce the problem clearly so that everyone understands it
- Identify possible solutions. Remember you will have given the problem more thought than anyone else
- Say what your preferred solution is, and why
- Invite discussion, and be open to hearing it and to re-assessing your position; a good constructive discussion speaks well of your introduction of the problem
- Make the decision and get consensus for it, if possible.

Easy? No, but it comes with practice and it feels good when it goes right!

Checking

Unfortunately it's no use just making decisions and telling, or persuading, people to implement them. You also have to check that what you instructed has actually been done.

Maybe it shouldn't have to be like that, but I'm afraid it is. Ignore it at your peril!

Choice

Try to give those who work for you choice in what they do. At first sight this sounds a little bizarre; you might fear that they will choose to do nothing. However, that would be giving too wide a choice. The idea is that, within the direction dictated by you, the person can choose which course he or she takes. The big advantage of this is that it increases the person's commitment – after all, if they themselves have chosen to do what they are doing, how can they fail to be committed?

What you are aiming for is that the people working for you feel as if they have chosen their course of action, even though you have dictated the overall direction. Some managers contrive to do exactly the opposite; *telling* people what to do, while failing to provide an overall policy.

See **Compliance versus acceptance**

Commonsense

Beware of commonsense; statements which have a 'ring of commonsense' *might* be good for convincing others, but do not be deceived by what those fond of jargon call 'face validity'.

One of the best examples of this was when John Peyton, who, some years ago, as Minister of Transport in the British government, was facing a hostile audience which was telling him how to make the roads safer. One member of the audience was hotly advising Mr Peyton that drivers with poor eyesight should not be allowed on the roads (surely a 'commonsense' safety measure). To his credit, Mr Peyton actually *cited evidence* which clearly demonstrated that, contrary to commonsense, shortsighted drivers are no more dangerous than those with sharp vision.

High fliers can distinguish facts from commonsense.

Compliance versus acceptance

Compliance is where, by means of the power that you have, you force your underlings to 'go along with' what you tell them to do (but they will be delighted if the plan goes wrong).

Acceptance is where you persuade and convince your underlings that what you are suggesting is the best course of action (therefore if the plan goes wrong, they will use their initiative to try and put it right).

Needless to say, we should always go for acceptance rather than compliance. One of the most famous examples of this was Churchill who is remembered, above all else, for his eloquent *persuasion* of the British people that his course of action was the right one.

Computer games, juggling and cricket

I heard recently of a course on coping with stress, on which the participants (all managers of various kinds) were taught how to juggle. Real juggling, that is, not juggling priorities.

This is not as daft as it sounds. It is quite a different activity from what we spend most of our working day doing . . . a quite different form of brain activity. But brain activity nevertheless. And it adds a balance to the intensive intellectual activity that makes up most of our working day. This doesn't only make life pleasanter for us, but actually enables us to work better and more enthusiastically.

Juggling is not the only activity like this, of course, hence the title. Go for the computer games that require lots of reaction-time type activity . . . not the intellectually stimulating ones! Never mind using your microcomputer entirely for spreadsheets, databases and wordprocessing, get expert also on what good games are available . . . there are some gems!

What do they say . . . 'All work and no play makes Jack a dull boy'? It's surprising what truth there is in these things sometimes . . . and I can't imagine that things are any different for Jill!

Consulting

Before making a decision, always work out who will be affected by the decision, and ask their advice. This way you will obtain their commitment if you go along with their advice and you will know what you are running into if you go against it. You will also have an opportunity of explaining your decision to them and, hopefully, getting them on your side.

See **Decisiveness**

Contaminating the decision

When you are deciding on a course of action, you specify the problem, generate some possible solutions, and then weigh up the pros and cons of each to determine what you should do . . . don't you?

It sounds very straightforward and effective doesn't it? But is it *really* what you do?

Many of us contaminate our decision-making process by concerning ourselves with how *feasible* the various options are, too early on.

Feasibility is vital, of course, but it should be the last factor to be considered. What one initially wishes to know is, 'What is the best decision, assuming all the options are feasible?' If it later turns out, after proper study, that your chosen option *really* is not feasible, or is too expensive, then you can go back and reconsider. Make sure you leave feasibility considerations to last – it will save you discarding some really good options.

Counter-control

This is the jargon term for banging one's head against a brick wall.

It is a simple notion: there are some people who, if you try to control them, will react by demonstrating how unwilling they are to be controlled. This means that, for such people, you have to get them on your side, you have to motivate them, you have to gain their commitment and enthusiasm. Given that, such people can be trump cards.

See Compliance versus acceptance, Blaming, 'One suggestion would be ..,' Optimism, 'I told them how to do it ..,' Lack of co-operation and Choice

A day's work

It was said of Harold MacMillan that he was a wonderful person to work for because he always got the day's work done within the day.

This is an important aim to achieve because:

- It makes you set realistic goals for a day
- It makes you feel good at the end of the day if you achieve what you intended
- It sets off the next day (and therefore every day) with the optimistic air of a new challenge.

Try to do it – it makes you feel good and, therefore, makes you work better, more optimistically and more energetically.

The way to achieve it, however, is not (simply) by staying late until it's all done, it is also by setting yourself realistic, achievable goals at the beginning of the day.

See *Reactive tasks* and *Self-esteem*

Delegation

Delegation does not come automatically; it is a skill that we have to learn. However, there are some pretty watertight rules to help us

- Use it to enhance your own job by giving you more time to do what you are uniquely good at, and to enhance your subordinates' jobs by giving them added responsibility and authority
- When you delegate a task, you do not 'wash your hands' of it; you make it plain to your subordinate that he or she is free to come back to you for advice at any time. In any event they should give a progress report from time to time. If they don't, you should check on how things are going. Encourage and congratulate (if appropriate!)
- Let others know that it is now your subordinate who is responsible for the task in question. This feels difficult, because it seems as if you are losing power and influence. Don't worry, it's not true.

Democratic decision making

Not a good way of making decisions because you will usually alienate a substantial minority of the group making the decision. They will produce justifications such as you not having taken into account the strength of their feelings as well as their number.

This kind of decision making is not time efficient either. For example, twenty well-paid National Health Service employees once spent half an hour deciding to leave a particular set-up as it was, with never any prospect that they would come to a different decision. This means that in the space of half an hour, ten man-hours, or substantially more than one working day, were wasted.

If you are paid to make decisions, consult others if needs be, and *then* make them. Remember to *sell* your decision; carry others with you.

Diary

We are not talking about your appointments diary here, but the book in which you record your 'daily reflections'.

The main functions of such a diary are to help you to assimilate events as they happen and to put them into an overall **perspective**. In other words, it keeps you on track, helps you see what you are doing right or wrong and generally acts as an all-purpose and absolutely discreet confidant.

Not a bad pay off for a few minutes 'work' each day. Keep a diary.

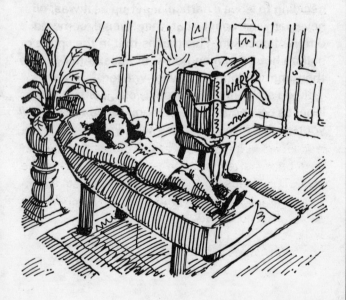

Diffusion of responsibility

This is what happens when you ask 'someone' to do a task. No one takes responsibility, no one does it. It is no one's fault. You *have* to name a specific person when you delegate a task.

This concept can lead to a substantial saving of person-power. All the training courses I organize are evaluated, and we have found that courses run by two people are, in general, not as successful as those run by one. This is strange, but good news, because it liberates 50 per cent of a highly skilled group to do other tasks and simultaneously results in a better 'product'.

One sometimes sees the same phenomenon where a 'sub-group' or 'study group' or 'sub-committee' is set up to examine a particular area. The results of some of these studies are so poor, and so out of line with the ability of some of the *individuals* in the group that it is plain that it would have been better to ask one person to tackle the task. This leads to a potentially vast saving in personnel *and* an improved result. You *can* have your cake and eat it!

See **Laws of physics**

Don't phrase things negatively (!)

It's depressing to hear what you shouldn't do. Why? Because it doesn't help us to improve.

So, use a little more effort, and think how to phrase things in the positive way. For example, instead of 'Don't be so aggressive in meetings' (which gives no useful instruction as to how you should behave), try 'You'd do better to listen to what others have to say, show that you've understood, and then say what you think.'

It takes a lot more thought on your part, of course, but at least you stand a chance of being effective. The other way, there is no chance.

Do the worst tasks first

When you are confronted by an array of tasks, all of which need doing at one point or another, which do you do first? Ideally, of course, you give them priorities, concentrating only on important tasks and starting with the most urgent of these.

But what if, somehow, you just can't get it together to do that, and it all seems a bit too much? *Start with the task you don't want to do!* Maybe it sounds crazy; maybe you think you should just have a coffee to 'warm up slowly' or start with some of the easy tasks to 'get yourself into gear' or whatever other phrase you have for it.

Forget that. Just start with the most awful task and you will find it works! Why should it work? Because the effect of completing this first, awful task – whether it's just a difficult phone call or whatever – is that you can get on to a more pleasant task. In other words, you are rewarded for that piece of work by being allowed an easier piece. (But remember each time to select the worst task as it gets progressively easier.)

Compare that with the alternative; that is, starting with the more inviting tasks and working towards the tricky ones. What is your pay off for completing those inviting tasks? The answer is, you land yourself with something you didn't want to do. The result? Even those formerly inviting tasks get tarnished and become progressively less inviting, and your work rate goes down.

The solution is to do the worst task first. That way, even the awful tasks somehow seem less awful and you're constantly (and speedily) heading towards the light at the end of the tunnel.

Executive toys

Executive toys include things like radio-pagers, car telephones, fancy office phones, and so on. Some people actually *need* these things. Even if you don't, there is no harm in them if they give you some fun.

There are a couple of dangers though. The first is that you gear your work to the gadgets you've got, and lose sight of your real goals. The second is that you bankrupt yourself buying these exotic playthings. They can be expensive!

Exercise

Yes, we all know that exercise is good, but it's difficult to get around to doing it regularly. And anyway, why should we?

Too much is made of exercise. In reality, it's easy to do and its benefits are clear . . . we feel better, we look better, and, importantly, we are more energetic as a result.

Sounds good so far. So what do we have to do to obtain all these wonderful pay-offs? Simple, we should take 20 minutes steady exercise at least every other day.

'Steady' means something like a purposeful walk. Use a cycling or rowing machine if you like, but take it easy. Don't work so hard at it that you put yourself off ever doing it again. Remember it only has to be 'steady'. 20 minutes means exactly that; 20 minutes all in one go, not two bouts of ten. No need to do more than twenty.

It's important to do it more or less exactly this way because it takes 20 minutes exercise to lead to a maintained raising of the metabolic rate. It stays relatively raised for about 48 hours.

Expert

The term *expert* has suffered much abuse over the years – so much so that it has become unfashionable to be, or even to consult, an expert. One even hears gross red herrings such as whether or not it is arrogant of a person to term themselves an 'expert'; this leaves aside the important question of whether an expert has knowledge that is worth using.

The answer is a simple one; if the person *really* is an expert in a matter that is relevant to you, then pay close attention to all that he or she has to say. However, be sure of the individual's credentials, and do not pay undue attention if he or she is talking in a field outside their area of expertise. Be in no doubt, though, real experts are a very valuable resource if they are experts in what you wish to know about.

Fear of failure

This concept is old hat, commonly ignored, and yet continues to be one of the most frequent and powerful notions to explain poor performance in normally high-achieving individuals.

The best example is with two sports teams competing at a high level, where the 'underdog' often performs the better of the two, because, for them, there is no failure to be fearful of – if they win it is a tremendous achievement, if they lose it is par for the course. For the favourites, the opposite is true – winning is par, losing is dismal failure.

In business, fear of failure is manifested less obviously, and most often rears its head in the form of avoiding or delaying a particular project.

The paradox:

- Many people don't attempt a task, for fear of failure
- What would happen if they do fail?
- They would be in exactly the same situation as if they don't attempt the task!

Always have a go!

Fudging

Fudging occurs when:

- You think one thing, the person you are talking to thinks something else
- You know this is the case though sometimes this knowledge is at the back of your mind
- You allow the misunderstanding to stand
- It stores up trouble for you both later.

Don't do it. Clear things up *now*. It will probably be worse later on!

Fun

We all work better when we are enjoying ourselves – we are more constructive, free-thinking, energetic and productive. That means that you must enjoy your work, and arrange it so that those around you enjoy it too. It is not *just* an attitude of mind; things need to be organized so that work is enjoyable, people have some jokes and generally feel good.

Making work fun does not *necessarily* mean organizing a good time over the lunch break, with trips to the pub or office parties in the evening time. In fact, these can sometimes act as compensation for what should really be happening: that the work itself is fun.

Gut reaction

Much over-rated – try thinking instead.

Holidays – the five basic rules

- Take them; they really do bring a sense of perspective to work
- Make sure you have an annual one of at least two weeks; it takes time to wind down
- Don't take work with you on holiday – a holiday *does not* mean doing your work in a different setting
- Make arrangements for your work to be done while you are away – there is no point in taking a holiday if you have to work twice as hard when you return
- Don't suddenly do strenuous exercise while you are away – a lot of business people die on their holidays

Indecision

Indecision causes stress. Indecision can be a chronic state where the individual hardly realizes that he spends half his time deciding what to do next; he knows that he is simply uncertain and unsure.

Paradoxically, the decision itself is sometimes quite unimportant. It is frequently the *commitment* to the decision that is vital. Often, it is not so much the action that you take, but the energy and enthusiasm that you put into it which count.

An individual and his actions

It is important to be able to criticize the actions of others. It is also important to have others permanently on your side. To do this you have to be able to convey two messages simultaneously:

- That you like or, at worst, are neutral to the individual to whom you are talking
- You disapprove of, or at least have reservations about, a particular *action* that that individual has taken.

There are various mechanisms for doing this, for example, your **tone of voice**, but perhaps most important is to have the distinction between an individual and his actions clearly in mind.

Interruptions

Do not curse interruptions or interrupters. If interruptions are an unavoidable part of your everyday work, make sure you leave time for them when you plan your day. Just because you don't know the specific form or time that an interruption will take, that doesn't mean that you shouldn't plan for it.

If the interruptions are *not* a proper part of your day, then find a system (other than snapping off the heads of the interrupters) of preventing them from happening. Routing them to the appropriate person is one of the more obvious solutions.

See **Reactive tasks**

'I told them how to do it'

People do not respond well to being *told* how to do something unless it is a mundane task. High fliers generally interact with people doing sophisticated tasks who have considerable autonomy. High fliers will therefore not be in the business of 'telling people how to do it'. If you do, you will be reducing **initiative** and dampening motivation.

A better approach is to *guide* by asking appropriate questions. A not particularly subtle sequence might be as follows:

- 'What do you reckon went wrong?'
- 'Would it have been possible to do things differently?'
- 'So tell me again, what are you saying you would do differently next time?'

Certainly by no means a subtle example, but equally certainly a lot better than *telling* your colleague what he or she should have done.

See **Lack of co-operation**

Job interviews –
phrases people use to
describe themselves

- 'I don't suffer fools gladly.'
  This means the candidate is an irritable, bad-tempered so-and-so
- 'I have a good sense of humour.'
  This means the candidate has no sense of humour at all
- 'I'm firm but fair.'
  This means the candidate is bossy and overbearing.

Keeping your
options open

Always do this, as long as it doesn't actually block you making a good decision or delay you making it.

There is little to be said in favour of **burning your boats** just for the sake of it.

171

Key questions

The director of a training course in clinical psychology once said that, although at the end of the course, trainees sat rigorous written examinations, there was, for him, one key question, namely, 'Is that person now good enough to treat a loved one of mine?'

It is a crucial point. If they are not good enough to treat one's own loved ones, then how can they be good enough to treat someone else's, no matter what exam results they have.

Every area has its own key question, it's just a matter of identifying them. Once you have done that, they are really obvious!

Lack of co-operation

When others do not seem to be co-operating with you, it is tempting to see them as straightforwardly bloody-minded. In reality, there are two possibilities: they may lack motivation (roughly akin to being bloody-minded), or they may simply be unable (rather than unwilling) to cope with what you asked them to do.

Plainly, if they lack motivation, you have failed to motivate them. If they are unable to do what you are asking, then the next question to ask is 'Do they have the aptitude for the task?' If they *do* have the aptitude, their training has been lacking. If they *don't* have the aptitude, they are in the wrong job, and you should either transfer them or seek to terminate their employment.

See Choice, Compliance versus acceptance, I told them how to do it and Optimism

Laws of physics

. . . have a lot to answer for. The problem is that people apply them to human and business relationships. An example: we talk about people 'letting off steam' with, at the back of our mind, the notion that it is good for a *boiler* to let off steam. Without doing so it explodes, after doing so it is more quiescent, its energy harnessed. The problem is that *people* don't literally let off steam: what we are referring to is someone shouting and bawling at another person, and this is rarely a good idea. What is more, the shouter/bawler does not by any means feel better afterwards. Generally, he or she feels extremely agitated.

The worst one, though, is about action and reaction being equal and opposite – you know the one where if a small bullet goes shooting forwards, the (relatively) big gun necessarily goes shooting backwards (into your shoulder). Without actually stating this law, the inappropriate conclusion that some people jump to is 'If he's getting something good out of his relationship with me, I must be losing out in some way.' This is just not true: the best and most stable (business) relationships are where both parties get plenty out of it, and there are plenty of these about. Think not only of competition but also of co-operation.

See **Compliance versus acceptance**

Leadership

If you are the head of an organization or a section in the organization, you should provide:

- A sense of direction
- Enthusiasm
- Inspiration.

This does not mean you have to be particularly outgoing; you can demonstrate these qualities in quite a low-key way. However, there is no avoiding the issue, these are the qualities you are trying to convey. Don't opt out for **fear of failing**. Better to make a half-successful attempt than no attempt at all.

Letters, typing and presentation

People judge you and your organization by (amongst other things) how well your letters and other written material are presented. If they see a letter from you that is poorly laid out, carelessly typed or carelessly composed then they will assume that this is typical of your organization.

Being a little more optimistic, this can work very well for you. A well-composed letter, well typed and well presented subtly suggests your efficiency and competence. This is, of course, a stroke of tremendous good fortune because it is a great deal easier to produce a well-presented letter than it is to have that same thoroughness throughout an entire organization. With a letter one can see straight away whether it is up to scratch and, if not, what is wrong with it and what needs to be put right.

Just like your appearance in general, the appearance of your letters and written material is very important indeed. Perfection is overrated, so don't worry about a third, fourth or fifth draft of your letter! On the other hand, make sure that a competent effort goes out neatly typed; doing that will say things that you can't say any other way.

See **Appearance** *and* **Perfection**

Luck

The conventional and correct wisdom is 'always back the lucky one'. The reason for this is that managers, like all people, are a mosaic of many different qualities and it is difficult, if not impossible, to see exactly why a manager has been successful in a specific situation. That is why one relies on 'past form', the 'track record' and the 'lucky one'.

Manner

It is important to be able to judge someone's manner when evaluating them.

A person's manner can be highly misleading; an individual with a warm manner is not necessarily friendly, he may be downright cynical; because he looks honest, he does not necessarily have integrity; because he talks confidently, does not mean he is necessarily competent.

Once we grasp that one's manner is different from one's personality, we are on the road to being able to assess these personality characteristics correctly.

Modesty

In everyday life, modesty is well thought of, particularly in others, as it means they are not openly competing with oneself. Thus one responds well to modesty in people such as authors and archaeologists, and one is prepared to contradict self-deprecating statements that these people make – sometimes.

However, there is another group of professionals for whom modesty is positively unwise. That group is the 'my' professionals; those people about whom a person would say to their friend, 'There is *my* architect' (or doctor, solicitor, etc.). In such cases, the client would not want to point out a scruffy individual in a battered Morris. Or another example, if one is consulting one's doctor, seriously concerned about one's health, one does not wish to hear him or her say that they are not really a very good doctor – one is not impressed by the modesty of such a statement.

Be careful of modesty!

Must

A nasty little word used destructively in two ways:

- To tell others that they *must* (or have to, or have got to) do something. Most people react to this by asserting, either overtly or surreptitiously, that they do *not* have to. Most people treasure their free will
- Some people use it to wind themselves up, as in 'I *must* sell x items,' or 'I *must* get the report finished this evening.'

Plainly, it would be nice if these things happened, but it is *not* the case that they *must* happen. Some people cause themselves undue **stress** and distort their thinking by telling themselves that such things *must* happen.

Names – forgetting them

If you forget someone's name in the course of a conversation cover it up – most people like to have their names remembered. There are two possible situations: temporary or permanent forgetting; both have similar strategies.

Temporary forgetting

Don't say, 'It is like Mr . . . (pause, desperately trying to remember his name) Smith was saying earlier.' This makes it obvious you had forgotten his name.

Do say, 'It is like Mr . . . (pause as though collecting thoughts, but in reality remembering his name). It's like Mr Smith was saying earlier.' In other words, start the complete sentence again.

Permanent forgetting

Start the sentence again, omitting the name completely (after all you have no option, you have forgotten it!) As in, 'It is like the very important point that was made earlier on,' as though your restart was in order to emphasize just how important the point was. Smith will be pleased!

Note-taking

Note-taking during interviews or conversations is a controversial issue. Some people robustly maintain that they *never* take notes during an interview, others that they *must* have it in writing. The advantages of note-taking are two-fold:

- You have a permanent record of what was said
- That by judicious timing of your note-taking you can give the impression (probably accurately) that you are taking what is said seriously thus helping to get the other person on your side.

The disadvantages of note-taking are probably well known:

- Note-taking gives the impression of a lack of **confidentiality**.
- Note-taking may inhibit the disclosure of information as it lends an air of formality to the proceedings.

See Putting it in writing

Optimism

Certainly a sight better than pessimism. Try to ally it with enthusiasm and enjoyment. All of these are infectious.

Pacing

Many people see their careers as a race, which is judged when they reach retiring age, when, so their unconscious tells them, all the status and material goodies they have acquired will be added up and assessed, and they will know how well they have done in the race. At last, they will feel good.

In reality, it is not like that. Each day, week, month has to be rewarding in its own right if you are to work in an enthusiastic and effective way.

What that means is *pacing* yourself so that you can maintain your energy levels right up to retiring age, and don't 'burn out' at 35, 40 or 45.

Paperwork

Get rid of it.

Partners

There is one important thing to remember when you are looking for a partner – that he or she should *not* be someone who is too similar to yourself; you are after somebody with complementary abilities to your own. After all, what is the point in recruiting somebody simply to duplicate your assets; you've got those already!

This sounds a little obvious but needs stating. Some managers use slightly bizarre methods for personnel selection, relying on 'chemistry', 'finding someone they can work with', and so on. All too often, they end up choosing someone who is similar to themselves.

Take the case of the managing director who used a firm of management consultants to help him select his financial adviser. The consultants warned him that their advised choice was his last choice, simply because that person was so different to him. It is perhaps worth mentioning the end of the story. The managing director accepted the consultants' advice, employed the financial adviser and was extremely pleased with 'his' choice.

Personnel selection

Both the selection and training of personnel are essential. If they are both essential, then how can one be more important than the other? Logically it cannot, but if it could, selection would be more important!

For example if you are responsible for negotiating the release of hostages whenever a plane is hijacked in Britain, you will need to select people with the aptitude for negotiating. Even so, they will need certain aims and objectives. Given that training, you will then have first-rate negotiators. But, if you select someone without aptitude, no amount of training will turn him or her into a negotiator. Such training is known as flogging dead horses, and is expensive.

Make sure you are up to date on selection procedures. Interviews are useless by themselves.

Persuasion

A necessary part in the implementation of a decision is to persuade people that you have decided on the right course of action. This is often overlooked by indecisive people trying to be decisive; these people tend to leap to conclusions and then simply issue instructions, in the futile hope that their underlings will be impressed by their virile 'decisiveness'. In fact, if one looks at leaders such as Churchill in the Second World War, many of his endeavours were directed at *persuading* the British people that the course of action that he was taking was the correct one.

See **Decisiveness** *and* **Relationships**

Playing to your strengths

Some people like to be up at five in the morning, working until breakfast and others like to sleep in the afternoon and then work into the early hours of the morning, while yet others work into the late evening at the office and don't touch work once they are home.

Find out which way suits you best, whether it is one of these or something entirely different, and have the courage to go for it. It is up to you to get the best out of yourself, and everyone has times of the day when they work best; everyone has their own rhythm.

The posh office

It is said that there is a inverse correlation between the poshness of head office and the efficiency of the organization. (The posher the office the less efficient the company.)

That might be taking it a bit far, although the opulence of the spectacularly-crashing Polly Peck's offices was notable. Better simply to register that plush surroundings are not essential to a thriving company. Let most of our daydreams centre around making the business a dynamic success. That way you won't need to convince others by more superficial means!

Positive and negative control

Positive control means influencing people's behaviour by praise, compliments, positive feedback and other pleasant consequences.

Negative control means influencing behaviour by nagging, issuing **threats**, grumbling and other unpleasant behaviour.

Generally speaking, especially if you require an individual to do a fairly sophisticated task, positive control is more effective. It certainly leads to lower **stress**, better morale, and greater commitment.

The reasoning behind the effectiveness of positive control is that one's staff are rewarded every time they do something well, so they do it well again, with the end result that, ultimately, there is little or no time for them to do anything badly.

Power

Whatever power you have, wield it in a way that makes people glad it's you that has it. That way you will keep it more easily.

Pressure interviews

These interviews used to be fashionable, mainly for selection. The interviewer would be deliberately antagonistic, rude and abrasive towards an individual, possibly putting him into awkward situations such as giving him a cigarette with no ashtray available. The excuse put forward for the interviewer's abominable behaviour is that it gives him a chance to see how the applicant responds to pressure.

Such procedures are, in reality, a thinly disguised excuse for sadism on the part of the interviewer. Rarely, if ever, is it possible to predict how an interviewee might react, for example, to the pressures of overwork, demanding colleagues or long hours from how he reacts to an abrasive interviewer in a job interview.

As an interviewer, have nothing to do with pressure interviews. As an interviewee, have nothing to do with any organization which subjects you to them.

Protest

There are times when even the best of people are helpless – maybe they are on the receiving end of a price hike from a monopoly supplier, maybe they're unfairly dealt with by a superior, maybe it's some other situation in which there is nothing they can do.

So what *do* you do? Do you sulk? Do you kick the cat? Do you simply slope off feeling frustrated and angry?

There is only one action that you can certainly take, and that is to protest. Loudly, urgently and vehemently if necessary, but not bitterly or pathetically. Then you learn what you can from the situation and get on with working constructively and enthusiastically again – even if it is for or with the person who has dealt with you unfairly. Sulking and sloping are rarely the stuff of high fliers!

Putting it in writing

The traditional purpose of 'putting it in writing' is, of course, to have an unequivocal record in case there is a dispute later. However, it also serves another, often overlooked, function – that of clarifying the thoughts of the writer.

It can therefore be used as a valuable timesaving technique, particularly, but not exclusively, when dealing with subordinates, in the following way. When a subordinate approaches you with something that has been 'preying on their mind', and then proceeds to work out their thoughts in a prolonged discussion, you should ask the subordinate 'to make a note of it'. The very act of attempting to write the matter down in a comprehensible form usually clears the subordinate's mind and the issue disappears. If the issue *is* an important one, writing it down will also be an advantage. Either way, you win.

Quiet time

Give yourself a quiet time every day, or at least, most days. This means getting your secretary to take all your calls for an hour (he or she can always contact you if it is absolutely essential!), making sure your door is uninvitingly shut, or even going off somewhere you won't be found, like a library or an empty office.

What do you do in that time? You almost certainly have a project which would benefit from some concentrated thought or some quiet writing; this is the time for such things. If you don't have anything like that, if all your time seems appropriately spent in a busy, interruptible office, then maybe you need to look carefully at how you spend your day!

Reactive tasks

These are the tasks that you forget to allow for when you are planning your diary – items like interruptions, incoming phone calls, things going wrong. These are the items which, because they haven't been allowed for, cause chaos in your diary/life/psyche and boost the degree of **stress** you feel.

The solution is simple. If you are putting a half-hour task in your diary, allow an hour for it. That way you will have a half-hour spare to deal to with the unexpected reactive tasks. (Just because you don't yet know what it's going to be, it doesn't mean it won't happen.) If, by good fortune, no reactive tasks appear, then have something important lined up to do – for example, a book or journal article which you need to read to keep your knowledge up to date,

Don't try to fool yourself into thinking that today will have no reactive tasks in store for you. It will, and you have to allow for them.

See Urgency and importance

Reserved spaces in the car park

Not an important issue in its own right, perhaps, particularly if you are one of the lucky ones who already has a reserved space. It is included in here as a example of the apparently innocuous issues that can blow up in your face without warning. Characterized by the **meeting** in which all the members sat dreamily through the chairman's exposition of how the organization had overspent by £23m on fuel costs in that year, but suddenly sprang rather aggressively into life when discussing the next item on the agenda, an application from one of the employees to have his name added to the reserved spaces list. Neither was it a passing issue – a senior member of the organization threatened to resign, several weeks later, if a reserved space were not found for him as well.

The key notion is that of status and prestige, areas that everyone is highly sensitive about, and that the people at the top should be aware of and devote some thought to.

Risky shift

The risky shift is a phenomenon whereby a group of people will take a significantly more risky decision than any one individual in that group.

It has also been observed that a group may take a decision that is foolhardily cautious or conservative. Indeed the same group may do both – take some excessively high-risk decisions and some excessively low-risk decisions.

Obviously this can have serious ramifications for an organization, and there is little one can do except to be aware of the phenomenon. There are various possible reasons for it, the favourites amongst which are 'the diffusion of responsibility', i.e., no one feeling personally responsible for the decision, and a simple reluctance to disagree with the group, for fear of being **'put down'**.

Scoundrels and vagabonds

Some people in the world are just plain stupid, wicked or idle.

It may be that you have done all the right things to manage an individual effectively, read all the right books, and generally worked yourself into the ground trying to get the best out of a particular individual.

If you are *absolutely* sure that the person concerned is virtually useless to you in any capacity, then you simply have to get rid of him or her. Certainly, human awareness and sensitivity are very valuable assets in your armoury, but so are the ability to appraise an individual's qualities objectively and the courage to follow the necessary course of action.

Secretaries – getting on with them

Your first priority at work should be to get on with your secretary. There are two reasons for this:

- It's hell if you don't, because you see so much of them
- People believe what they are told about you by your secretary. They believe that this is the 'real you', so it's as well to make sure that what they hear is good.

'Seeking a fresh challenge'

This is a cliché trotted out by someone leaving a job for whatever reason. However, you really benefit by setting yourself a new challenge every couple of years or so, maybe by moving job, maybe by reconstructing your existing one.

If you settle into a routine of using a particular set of abilities, you forget you have others that you are not using, or you do not develop new ones. If you haven't moved or completely restructured things for a long while, you will be amazed how a shake up will brighten you up, even if you reckon you are pretty bright already! If you have been in your current situation for significantly more than two years, give this some very serious thought.

Self-esteem

As a general rule, people perform better when they think well of themselves. This means that we should try to boost the self-esteem or self-confidence of our colleagues or subordinates. This has a side effect: those people will usually come to think better of us as well, and do a little PR on our behalf.

The best way to boost the self-esteem of others is:

- To give the individual *sincere* compliments, being sure to stick to those areas where you can genuinely compliment the person concerned
- To get your colleague to say what he or she has done well or is particularly pleased with – it sounds odd, but can easily enough be done with either casual conversational remarks such as 'Tell me some good news' or in more formally organized feedback sessions. Make sure you say you agree (if you do) when your colleague is bold enough to tell you their strengths!

Whatever you do, stick to *sincere* compliments, and remember to keep up your *own* self-esteem – remind yourself of the things you have done well.

See **Feedback** *and* **Self-efficacy**

Setting limits

Many people unwittingly set limits for themselves. In their heart of hearts they don't believe they should be *too* successful – they feel they should just have a 'respectable' degree of success, combined with a decent degree of modesty.

If that is what you really want, that's okay, so long as you recognize it. If not, and you want all the success you can possibly achieve, then just make up your mind what you mean by success and go for it. Take off the unconscious brakes.

Shoes

Shoes are the best guide to a person's wealth and personality. Good clothes now are cheap enough for virtually everyone to afford; one can buy, quite cheaply, a suit that is good enough not to be distinguishable from a much more expensive article to the untrained eye. Shoes are a different matter. Not only can most people spot the difference between cheap and expensive shoes, but they are also, literally, a walking personality test. One can hazard a pretty good guess, from looking at someone's shoes, whether they are what they seem, and you can tell the characteristics of robustness, fussiness, pretentiousness, flashiness, subduedness, conformity, etc.

Silence

Use silence with caution, as some people can't tolerate it nearly as well as others.

Some people use silence to 'draw people out'. Do this with caution, as sometimes people will say things they do not believe, simply in order to break a silence.

Sleeping on it

'Sleeping on it' is fine: some decisions really are complicated; they have aspects to them which do not occur to you straightaway and they do need you to mull them over.

The mind functions in quite a different way depending on the situation, so the chances are that you will see a problem in one light when you are at your desk, actively poring over it, and in quite a different light if you are to give it the occasional thought when you are driving home or having a drink with a friend. However, bear in mind that the point of delaying a decision in this way is *not* simply to **procrastinate**, it is to give it further thought in a different setting and come to a conclusion by the next day. If the problem is not complicated or important, then get it out of the way immediately.

Solemn and serious

Just a little clarification of these two, which are often confused. The key fact is that to be serious, you do not necessarily have to be solemn.

Some people are shocked if they see a surgeon laugh or crack a joke during an operation. Wrongly, they believe that they are not taking their job seriously. They are of course; they are simply not performing it solemnly. Frequently, the lessening of tension in this way actually *improves* the quality of work, and this is so in the everyday jobs most of us do.

See Fun

Stress

Stress is bad news. It saps your **energy**, impairs your efficiency and effectiveness, and has been implicated in a range of serious physical ailments such as ulcers, heart attacks and even some forms of cancer.

There is nothing good to be said about stress, and you need to avoid the trap of thinking that because you feel stressed you are working hard and, therefore, doing a good job. If you are feeling stressed, you are almost certainly working below peak efficiency. You should aim to work hard but feel unstressed.

The basis of stress-avoidance is two-fold.

- *Be kind in what you say to yourself.* There is nothing intrinsically stressful about working late at the office – the stress comes when you say to yourself such as, 'Why the hell is it always me that gets landed with these jobs ... isn't it about time someone else did the donkey-work?' and so on. Learn to spot when you are winding yourself up and learn to be a little kinder to yourself. Talk to yourself as politely as you would when you talk to a friend or colleague.
- *Keep an eye on your physiology.* Really, this means keep relaxed, or if you need to, learn to relax. If you know that you are prone to be tense

when you don't need to be, then get yourself a relaxation cassette tape to listen to every day – there are plenty of good tapes about, or even go to relaxation classes in the evenings – you will probably find it is time well spent. As well as this, get regular, steady exercise at least every other day – 20 minutes walking is just about ideal.

See **Fitness**

Threats

Some managers like to manage by encouraging and praising all the excellent things that their colleagues have done, others by pointing out people's mistakes and issuing threats, either openly or by their **tone of voice**.

In reality, people work best when they receive both praise *and* constructive criticism. Threats are nearly always counter-productive.

The worst offender in this respect is the person who issues threats which no one believes, or frequently talks in a threatening kind of way. This is the worst of both worlds: it wears down **relationships** and simultaneously fails to motivate people to avoid unpleasant consequences.

So, threats and threatening are to be avoided, but there is a cousin of threats that can be useful. This is the technique of simply spelling out to people in a neutral kind of way, what consequences will happen from particular courses of action. This enables people to make their own **choice**.

*See **Positive and negative control** and **Feedback***

Training films/books

Try to get into the habit of seeing training films and reading training books. A lot of people are sceptical about their value, but this is usually because they misunderstand their role. The key to success here is to have *realistic* expectations about what you can get out of a film or book. If you watch a film and find that every idea in it is new to you, then there is probably something seriously wrong with the way you are doing your job (or something seriously wrong with the training film). A realistic expectation might be to identify just *one* idea that strikes you as a good one, and which can also be applied when you get back to your office. It is better to identify and apply *one* idea than to appreciate a multitude of good ideas, but apply none.

Trust your staff

Regard your staff as a resource, not an expense.
You should be extremely thorough in staff selection, but once you employ them, you trust them, work for them, and do your best for them so that they are able to do their best for you. There will be a few who take advantage of such an attitude, but, overall, you will gain much more than you lose. Beware of self-fulfilling prophecies: if you don't trust your staff, you will eventually find that they are not trustworthy – they slack and don't do their best for you. If, on the other hand, you demonstrate that you work for them by, for example, getting them the best tools to do the job, you stand a better chance of most of you ending up on the same side!

Voting

. . . is okay at large meetings but divisive at small ones.

Walking the job

Walking the job means getting out of your nice plush office and literally walking around wherever you work, seeing and being seen by those who work for you. Who knows, you might even speak to them!

The benefits of this are two-fold. On the one hand, you get to know all sorts of information that you otherwise would not; not only do people mention certain things to you which they otherwise wouldn't bother, but you also see things going on which you won't see from the comfort of your office. Your subordinates will also realize that you are interested in what is happening and this will benefit morale.

If you walk the job, there will be no need for quips such as 'What is the difference between the Abominable Snowman and the managing director? . . . You see the Abominable Snowman more often.' You should never be too high and mighty to get out of your office and see what is going on for yourself.

Work is more fun than fun

A neat saying, reputedly one of Noel Coward's. An important one too, because it points out the fact that really successful people do not think of their work as work, but more as fun, a hobby, an interest. This is not to say that they don't put the hours in; just the opposite, when *they* take work home, they take it home and enjoy doing it. And if you enjoy doing something, you can go at it for a long while.

Treating work as enjoyment means that you bring optimism, cheerfulness and vigour to it while still putting in long hours. It's fun, *and* it cuts down on stress.

Exercises

Exercise 1   217
Exercise 2   218
Exercise 3   220

Exercise 4   221
Exercise 5   222
Exercise 6   233

Exercise 1

Write down the three concepts that are most relevant to you. For example, if you feel you should be more ambitious, more assertive and question your assumptions more, then write those three in the spaces here. Make sure that those you write are the three that are the most relevant to you *and* that you are keen to work on them.

1.

2.

3.

Exercise 2

Read through the example below, then go on to the next page and fill in the blank boxes.

Goal 1

To be more assertive

Steps to achieving this goal

- Prepare for meetings more thoroughly, canvassing opinion beforehand, and putting my point of view.
- Revise my strategy during meetings. I won't say so much, but will think out more carefully what I want to say, and say it at the right moment.
- In everyday interactions, I will state if I am annoyed/irritated etc., say what the person has done to make me feel that way, and ask them to behave in a particular other way. I will do that in a warm/friendly, but definite way, to those both above and below me in the hierarchy.

Frequency and method of reviewing progress

Every Friday at 5 p.m., for the next four weeks, I will run through the week and jot down examples of where I've succeeded, and also how I could have done better.

Goal 1
(taken from Exercise 1)

Steps to achieving this goal

Frequency and method of reviewing progress

Exercise 3

Make a note in your diary to do Exercise 4 in one month. *Do not read any further till then.*

Exercise 4

Repeat the exercise for your second goal from
Exercise 1.

Goal 2

Steps to achieving this goal

Frequency and method of
reviewing progress

Exercise 5

Make a note in your diary to do Exercise 6 in one month. *Do not read any further till then.*

Exercise 6

Repeat the exercise for your third goal from Exercise 1.

Goal 3

Steps to achieving this goal

Frequency and method of reviewing progress

A note

I hope you have enjoyed reading these entries and will work on them.

If you want to write and tell me which you found especially useful, or put forward ideas to be included in further volumes of Climbing the Corporate Ladder, please do so care of Thorsons, HarperCollins*Publishers*, 77-85 Fulham Palace Road, Hammersmith, London W6 8JB.

William Davies